Readymade Speeches and Debates for All Occasions

GOODWILL'S

Readymade Speeches and Debates for All Occasions

By

Madan Sood

GOODWILL PUBLISHING HOUSE®

B-3 RATTAN JYOTI, 18 RAJENDRA PLACE

New Delhi - 110 008 (INDIA)

Published by:

GOODWILL PUBLISHING HOUSE®

B-3 Rattan Jyoti, 18 Rajendra Place
New Delhi–110 008 (INDIA)
Tel: 25820556, 25750801, 25755559
Fax: 91-11-25764396
Email: goodwillpub@vsnl.net
ylp@bol.net.in
Website: www.goodwillpublishinghouse.com

Printed at : Kumar Offset Printers, Delhi-92

Preface

A fine orator can leave a great and an unprecedented influence on his audience. He can motivate the listeners according to his will, and can set the listeners' thinking in the direction he wants. He can mould their thinking.

Many professional skills depend on the power of speech. Hypnotic speech power makes the lawyers win cases, salesmen sell their products and the leaders rule over their subjects. The preceptor turns the minds of his disciples to veracity. The professor wins the hearts of his students and the extraordinary orator makes the audience oblivious of their surroundings. He can turn people's minds on the righteous path.

A speaker should have the speech ready. However, a born orator veers from documented words, merges his heart and soul in his speech and gives vent to his feelings, his obsession, his verve and creates the fireworks, the sparks of which reach every heart and soul.

Every speaker has his own method to reach his audience and his public. In order to ensure that his image stands unique, he has to bring out his originality through his speech.

This book contains readymade speeches on a variety of topics related to different spheres of life. After having gone through the book carefully, one can speak extempore on any topic of general as well as special interest. Besides, there are very important debates on issues of socio-economic concern which will be highly useful for students, professionals and people from all walks of life.

Madan Sood

Contents

SECTION I

Introduction

A speech is different from other compositions as it uses more of colloquial words. It is a formal talk that a person gives to his audience. An essay or composition uses formal words and if it is read as a speech, it cannot be regarded as a proper speech but at best a message. A written expression can be read again and again but in the case of a speech, the words uttered mostly melt in the air unless treasured in the minds of the listeners.

Literally, a speaker has to stress his points to convince his audience. In order to repeat his words and points, he has to resort to rhetoric, alliteration and dramatisation. It is not the dramatisation of his points of view but his logic and reasoning accompanied with intonation and enthusiasm that ensure the essence of his speech and set the listeners' thinking in the direction the speech attempts to.

A speaker has to have some basic training in speech making. However, it is not the kind of training one gets in a classroom. If one has interest and will to become an orator, one should begin by listening to speeches, by attending meetings, seminars, conferences and gatherings where the speakers deliver speeches.

A beginner may assess which speeches are impressive and which are not, following which he can analyse why some speeches are more impressive than others. He can weigh the effects of the uttered words. Then he can practise mock speech in his room and his resounding words would tell him what effects his words would have on the listeners.

Some orators are born with an inherent capacity to make speeches. Others can follow their footsteps and become great orators by listening them. One must identify oneself with the subject or topic on which one is going to deliver the speech. Speech may also be learnt by heart. But, when the same words are reproduced, it cannot be called an impressive speech. However, in delivering even the learnt speech, one is so much involved with it that, one is likely to utter different words and one's changed intonation and expressions, accompanied with one's postures will have a great impression on the audience.

In a debate, a person has to either support the issue or firmly oppose it. He is supposed to stick to his points and defend his stand; he cannot take up a position in-between. However, while delivering a speech, he can choose a middle path. But in that case he has to present both the sides in a logical manner.

For instance, while speaking on the topics like 'emerging culture of free mixing of boys and girls', or 'the good and bad points of divorce', the speaker can blend the pros and cons of the concerned issue and conclude that the mixing of boys and girls in moderation would take the steam off their curiosity and pave the way for the healthy growth of their personalities. Similarly, a divorce, may be good to save a woman's life and may provide her an opportunity to live in peace. However, the speaker must, first of all present the extreme merits and demerits in both cases. The main objective of a speech is to produce lasting effect on the audience. A speech may have a deeper and lasting effect on the audience if it is replete with the logic and reasoning along with the illustrations of day-to-day life and not by the unnecessary shouts and dramatics. Indeed it is ultimately logic and reasoning and not the intonation, expressions and enthusiasm of the speaker that hold the attention of his audience and create a soul-stirring effect. Deep and lasting effects are created by a speech which not only has the speech-histrionics, but is also backed by sound reasoning and arguments.

❑ ❑ ❑

SECTION II

Speeches on Ceremonies

Welcoming a New Incumbent

(Speech by Union Leader)

Mr Chairman, ladies and gentlemen!

It gives me a great pleasure to announce that Mr Robert is going to take over as our new General Manager. On this day, on behalf of the whole staff of our

company, I welcome him to our organisation. I hope that our organisation is sure to receive a great boost under the able guidance of Mr Robert who possesses unprecedented qualities of head and heart. Mr Robert, besides being highly qualified, has vast experience in diverse fields. Above all, he is a good team leader who has been instrumental in reviving many sick industries both in India and abroad. Such units are now making tremendous profits and thus contributing to the growth of economy.

As ours is a viable company, we have no problem of efficiency. Hence, it is earnestly hoped that Mr Robert after he takes over our organisation, will certainly prove to be a great asset to our company. We can expect enhanced profits and hence workers and employees of this organisation can expect more financial benefits in the form of hiked bonus and salary. However, gentlemen, I would like to make a point here that the impression should not go to anyone that we are working in this company solely for our returns and gains. Our main consideration, as the staff of the company, is the growth of the organisation. There is no doubt that if the company runs well and makes profits, we are sure to prosper.

Gentlemen, Mr Robert, would be the right person at the helm to guide the destiny of our organisation and staff and we are sure that it would be a great experience to work under his able leadership and efficient guidance.

Gentlemen, I may add here that we shouldn't only expect wonders and miracles from Mr Robert who is a human being like the rest of us. We can expect results from him only if we extend to Mr Robert our complete cooperation and assist him in the direction he is heading for the growth of the company.

Our faithful allegiance to Mr Robert and our commitment to work and duties will, no doubt, go a long way in making our organisation a viable and progressive one. I, on behalf of the staff, assure our new General Manager that we shall leave no stone unturned in extending our whole-hearted cooperation to him. All our sincerity and cooperation are with him in his endeavours to take this organisation to a new height of growth.

I, on behalf of the staff, extend the heartiest felicitation to Mr Robert.

Thank you.

❑ ❑ ❑

Farewell Speech
(Speech by Seniormost Staff)

Mr Chairman, respected General Manager, department managers, ladies, gentlemen and dear colleagues!

I am here to speak to you today with a heavy heart as we have gathered to bid farewell to Mr Darcy. Mr Darcy has been with us for more than two decades and has tremendously contributed to the growth of this organisation. In fact, it was his honesty, devotion, sincerity, integrity and commitment to work which have taken the organisation to a new height of growth.

By virtue of his qualities of head and heart, Mr Darcy has proved that for him duty is always before self, that work is worship and that completion of work one is assigned to accomplish, gives one great inner solace. Indeed he has a passion to work. Hence, he has been

a great inspiration to all of us all these years. Working with him is a great experience.

As you all know that partings and meetings are the inevitable realities of life and we cannot avoid them in spite of our best efforts. It is the law of nature that if we meet, we must part sooner or later whether we meet a fellow human being, a friend, a relative or some colleagues in a small or big organisation. Same is the case today when we are parting with Mr Darcy.

However, one comes across many persons during the span of one's life. Every individual has his distinct chracteristics. One may meet persons possessing all positive and healthy characteristics—persons who are generous, kind, helpful, selfless, non-partisan, devoid of snobbery, ego, haughtiness, arrogance or one may come across persons of negative traits—domineering, selfish, arrogant, self-centered and non-caring. We like to remember them by the qualities they possess.

Hence, we can never forget a person who possesses many good qualities of head and heart. In fact, we always cherish the memories of such a person even if he is no longer working with us. Mr Darcy has not only been a dedicated worker but a perfect example of human and humane qualities. His advice, help and cooperation extended towards his colleagues has worked miracles on many occasions and helped them in coming out of the tensed situation.

Our younger staff have always looked on him as a father-figure for whom he has been a mentor and guide and to the older employees he has been the universal 'brother Darcy'.

Now the time has come to bid a farewell to Mr Darcy because if we keep him with us for more time for our own inspiration and guidance, we won't be doing justice to him. We have to bear the loss of his great guidance, inspiration and unblemished support. In fact, parting with such a nice person, that to after a long association, makes one emotional, and which is quite natural, but this is destined, this has to happen.

Mr Darcy now needs rest, peace and realisation of the fruits of his labour. In the evening of his life, he requires calm, quiet and worry-free time.

It is heartening to announce that the retirement benefits and social security accumulations would afford Mr Darcy enough returns per year to retire from the hustle and bustle of life and live quite a contented life.

While bidding Mr Darcy a farewell, I would like to mention here that though he may be out of our working circle, he will never be out of our minds. His patience, perseverance, hard work and dedication would continue to guide us through the rough patches of time. We would always like to welcome Mr Darcy whenever he so desires. He is welcome to energise us and refresh himself as well with our company.

Let us all give Mr Darcy a big hand.

❑ ❑ ❑

Birthday Party
(Speech by a Relative)

Ladies and gentlemen!

I invite your kind attention on this auspicious occasion of the sixteenth birthday of Estella. The day of one's birth is a very crucial day. A new life comes into this world which is very uncertain. Like the uncertainty of this world our lives are also very uncertain. Sometimes one's life is filled with joys and ecstasies and sometimes one has to face many hardships and sorrows in life. All this is destined by the Almighty Whose will prevails in all our lives. However, it is very important that one should always be smiling and facing all odds with happiness and live life to the hilt.

I wish Estella many happy returns of the day! Being

her father's sister, I have seen Estella from the day she came into this world. I also remember her first birthday, her second birthday and all birthdays after that till today. In fact, I have seen her growing.

She has today stepped into her sixteenth birthday—the sweet sixteen in a girl's life. I wish her great happiness and success in life! I wish that she should sail through life with all the blessings of God. Ladies and gentlemen, please give Estella a big hand.

Before Estella blows out sixteen candles on her cake and cut the cake to mark the first day in her sixteenth year, I would like to say that she has excelled in life in all the fields. Besides being a good student, she has achieved tremendous success in sports and games as well. Recently she has bagged 'all rounder' medal in the inter-school tournament.

Since Estella is at the crossroads of life, I pray to God to give her enough strength and courage so that she can continue to keep up this spirit of excellence all through her life in her work and all other activities. I hope that she will be quite aware of her duties and responsibilities and will have all courage and determination to make a mark in life.

Estella has enough time to think and decide about the shape of things in her life. However, today we should forget rest all and rejoice in our thoughts that she has come of age. As the spotlight is on her, we should all lend our share to make this moment immensely happy for her. Best of luck to Estella! May you have always smile on your face! Good luck!

Happy Birthday once again!

❑ ❑ ❑

Birthday Celebrations
(Speech by a Close Friend)

Ladies and gentlemen!

At the outset, I wish my friend Rafique, many happy returns of the day! I would like to make you all know that I and Rafique are friends. We are childhood friends and Rafique and I grew up together and thus his life is an open book for me. We have studied together in school and in college. After the completion of education at college, Rafique then went to university to seek higher education. I turned to my family business.

The consistent and sturdy friendship of Rafique has always inspired me in my life. Whenever I was in pensive mood, he was always by my side to give me uplift needed and lift my spirits. He has always motivated me to have good thoughts and actions.

Through all these years, I have observed the fine mettle he is made of. In fact, it was only his inspiration

that saw me through the college. But for his inspiration I would have discontinued my studies in the college. I was on the verge of leaving college and joining the group of dropouts for my family was faced with financial crunch. I was not able to bear the expenses of my studies. Rafique extended all moral and financial support to complete my studies. I will remain indebted to him for the whole of my life.

I have no doubt that he will establish a firm niche in his life even if he has to face the toughest challenges. He is a man of high spirit. He is not a sort of fellow who would yield in the face of tough situation. In fact, he has the ability and skill to be the master of problems instead of allowing the problems to be his master. He possesses the ability to excel in any field. He has always been in the front row whether it is sports, studies, debates or extra curricular activities. Whatever he does, he does with full sincerity, commitment, dedication and devotion. He is well aware of his duties and responsibilities.

I wish him all the success in his life on this joyous occasion. May the Almighty make him successful in his career and also in his family life! I have firm faith that he will prove to be a good human being.

Ladies and gentlemen and dear friends, let us join in the rejoicings to extend our best wishes for a happy and successful life of Rafique. Long life, joy and prosperity to Rafique. Give him a big hand.

Thank you.

❑ ❑ ❑

Diwali Celebrations

(Speech by the Secretary of the Residents' Welfare Association)

Ladies and gentlemen!

Our local community has organised Diwali celebrations and I welcome all of you to participate in the celebrations. As you all know, Diwali is the festival of lights and on this day we decorate our homes, shops and all other working places with lights. All buildings are illuminated on this day, and present a wonderful sight.

Yes, the whole atmosphere is charged with festivities. We all are in a mood to enjoy. We wear new clothes and exchange sweets and gifts with our relatives and friends. We forget all our discords at least for one day. The festival brings us closer to one another.

Before the commencement of cultural programme and starting of fireworks, I would like to take you a few hundred centuries back. According to Indian epic, the *Ramayana*, Lord Rama, the righteous and virtuous son of Dashratha, the King of Ayodhya, returned after fourteen years of banishment in the forest. In this predicament Lord Rama was accompanied by his beloved wife Sita and his loyal brother Lakshmana.

Rama, Sita and Lakshmana had many escapades during this period of fourteen years. Lord Rama had to fight a battle with Ravana, the King of Lanka, and his powerful brother, Kumbhakarna and the great warrior Indrajit. Finally, Rama got victory over Ravana, who was killed along with many of his relatives and warriors. Lord

Rama returned to Ayodhya after crowning Vibhishana the King of Lanka. Vibhishana was the brother of Ravana but had left Ravana and joined Lord Rama for he was not happy with the evil designs of Ravana.

Lord Rama returned to Ayodhya, his kingdom, along with his wife Sita and brother Lakshmana. Diwali is celebrated to commemorate homecoming of Rama, Sita and Lakshmana to Ayodhya. On this day the city of Ayodhya was decorated with lights. This is the legend behind 'Diwali'.

Diwali celebrations coincide with the worshipping of Lakshmi, the goddess of wealth and goddess Kaali who had destroyed and eliminated evil from the face of the earth. Thus, Diwali marks the victory of good and virtuous over evil and vice. We are meeting here to invoke the spirit of truth and justice, happiness and co-existence on this earth.

We celebrate this festival with lights, crackers, exchange of presents and pleasantries to usher in the air an atmosphere of love, brotherhood, gaiety and prosperity.

So, ladies and gentlemen please participate in our celebrations to make them a community success.

May God always triumph over evil!

Religious Ceremony
(Speech by Pope)

Dear friends!

You all know that we all have congregated here to celebrate Christmas. As we all know religion is a way of life. It teaches us the norms, ethics and morals which we must follow in our lives to sail through difficulties and even ruins without grudging or carrying an adverse effects on our hearts and minds. In fact, religion guides us to righteous path. It is incumbent on all of us to remember the troubles and tortures the Great Saviour of mankind underwent and the sacrifices he made to redeem the human race from evil. Our sufferings will, no doubt, appear to be negligible if we compare them with those undergone by our Lord and Master. He was able to bear the deep sorrows and agonies without any grouse or grudge.

Of course, we are not here to do comparisons, but to propagate the teachings of our Lord and refresh our memories as well.

No religion teaches violence, hatred to mankind and ill-will or rancour for fellow beings. It is the human being who exploits religions to serve his selfish ends and makes the use of religion to grind his own axe and misleads innocent persons to fulfil his own nefarious designs. Truely, all men on this earth are not exploiters. However, a few who get the opportunity to exploit the religious feelings of their fellow human beings do so and go to the hilt to achieve their personal motives. They are so blind with their purpose that they can go to any extent in the name of religion. In fact, they use religion as a tool to serve their evil ends. All religions teach brotherhood, non-violence and love for all beings whether they are human beings or animals. Therefore, we should follow the tenets, advice and teachings of our Master. This would be the greatest reverence we can manifest to our Great Master.

The aim of our lives on this earth is to better ourselves by enriching and developing our minds and to do good to others. If we can develop ourselves physically, mentally and spiritually, we shall acquire enough confidence and we would be able to do our duty properly and guide and help others by providing assistance, help and moral support to them.

Let us all pray together on this auspicious day for the betterment of our bodies, minds and souls and take vows together that each day we shall do some righteous deed towards the welfare of mankind and extend all help to the needy, poor, downtrodden and deprived.

Amen!

❑ ❑ ❑

Marriage Anniversary
(Speech by an Invitee)

Ladies and gentlemen!

It gives me immense pleasure to speak on the fourth marriage anniversary of Mrs and Mr Andrews.

I congratulate Mrs and Mr Andrews on behalf of all those who are present here.

It is said that marriages are arranged in heaven and celebrated on the earth. We see today that many marriages break down a few days or months after they are solemnized. This is mainly attributed to the lack of patience and compatibility among the couples. A lot of tolerance, perseverance and sacrifice are needed to make a marriage successful.

It may take quite some time before the newly-married couples are able to understand each other and finally

settle down as a happy married couples. In this fast-paced life, there are many pressures—from the friends, parents, society, and pressures at work places—and many others which create several impediments in making marriages happy and successful. However, if the will of the Almighty prevails, most of the marriages will certainly turn out to be successful.

Dear friends, if you recall, it was really a very happy occasion for all of us when we attended the marriage of these love-birds. We had then noticed, with great joy, that they had eyes for only each other and no one else.

I hope my friend Andrews and Mrs Andrews will forgive me for making mention of this. However, I made a mention of this for the purpose to drive home the point to all the friends present here that we should pray to Almighty that all married couples may be blessed with love in their marriage.

Friends, our happiness knew no bounds when we noticed great love, care and concern extended toward each other on their first marriage anniversary and I can say for sure that this bond of love, trust and confidence between them has strengthened with the passage of time. This is really a matter of great pleasure. We all are really very happy to notice the ecstasy in their married life. On very rare occasions these days do we find the persistence and continuity of love among married couples after years of married life.

Love is the foundation of marriage and with such a married couple as the Andrews among us, we feel elated and satisfied. This marriage was further blessed with their first born, their darling daughter. There is no doubt that the nears and dears and very close friends of the Andrews found contentment to see them finally settle down in family life. We can see the couple blooming out perfectly on this fourth anniversary. They are spreading out the petals of married life. I, on behalf of you all present here, wish the couple incessant and lasting ecstasy in their married life forever.

I pray to God to shower the couple with all His blessings so that I along with my family and friends continue to come and enjoy the celebrations every year, on this date. I, with my family and friends, wish them, "Many many happy returns of the day!"

Thank you.

❑ ❑ ❑

Marriage Engagement
(Speech by a Close Relative)

Ladies and gentlemen!

It is a very auspicious day today, as we have been treated to a very pleasant surprise by Mr Arthur. The cause of great joy and surprise is the announcement by Mr Arthur that his daughter Adella is engaged to be married to Williams who happens to be a young pilot.

Being her uncle, I am proud to say that Adella is a gem of a girl. Adella not only possesses physical beauty but she is also endowed with brains. All along her academic performance in school and college, she has been an excellent student topping in more or less all the subjects. Hence, there is no doubt that Williams is a very lucky person to have Adella as his wife—a combination of beauty and brains.

As one of her closest relatives and uncle, I am, no doubt, pained to visualise that Adella will be leaving her family and friends and embarking on her journey towards a new life. At the same time, it is a matter of great pleasure that she is going to have her life partner—a nice man like Williams.

Such an occasion is a blend of greatest joy and deepest sorrow—sorrow to realise that the day of parting with the daughter is not very far, and joy because the daughter is going to settle in her married life. However, as a near and dear of the family, I have no hesitation to speak out my heart that my joy knows no bounds on the thought that our dear Adella is going to start her own family life. I wish her all the best and extend my heartiest congratulations to brother Arthur on this occasion.

Before the actual marriage takes place, the ceremony of engagement has great importance. This is the time when two young souls are publicly marked for each other. The sensitiveness of this period, the romance and the dreams between engagement and marriage are all unique. I bless Adella and Williams to experience great joy and bliss during this period. May the betrothed couple feel and live this period with great expectations and joy!

If we have positive thoughts in our mind and if we know how to face all odds and ups and downs of our life, the journey to life becomes easier and full of happiness. Adella and Williams are educated, well groomed and they will certainly brave all the problems of married life courageously. I, on behalf of all those present here, extend my best wishes to both of them. I request ladies and gentlemen to give them a big hand.

Thank you and have a great life ahead.

School Annual Function
(Speech by the Principal)

Honourable guests, respected parents, teachers and students!

Like the previous years, we have arranged to celebrate the Annual Function of our school this year too. Today is a very important and auspicious day for our school.

If I look back at the year gone by, I rejoice to say that I feel greatly elated and ecstatic to announce the achievements of our school made in different fields of activities and this gives me immense satisfaction.

Our meritorious students have held high the name of our school academically. Many such students have been placed in the merit list of the School Final Examination.

Many of our students have got admission in prestigious colleges in India on scholarships from the Board of

School Final Examinations of our state. Many have got scholarships in the colleges in which they were admitted. Majority of the students have been awarded scholarship from one or the other organisation. There are only four students who could not get the scholarships. However, our school is providing them promotional scholarships for one year so that they can be motivated in their further studies and make their career.

If I come back to the activities of our school, I find great pleasure to announce that the teaching system in the school has been upgraded and improved to keep pace with the fast changing education scenario and also to equip the students with necessary skills and capabilities to face the challenges of real life. In addition, our school has brought about a change in its policy to help those students who are meritorious but poor and deprived hence unable to afford the expenses of education.

Our students have excelled in extra-curricular activities too. They have won the inter-school hockey championship and were the runners-up in inter-school football tournaments. Our school won the inter-school quiz competition last year. In inter-state debate competition, our school held second position.

All sorts of outdoor and indoor games have been introduced by our school. And I hope that students will show their talents in the cultural programme that they are going to present before you this evening. They will also stage a play to add to the attraction of the programme. So, ladies and gentlemen, stay with us to enjoy and also to encourage our students this evening, and with your active participation and encouragement, I am sure, the students continue to give their best in all the activities they do.

Thank you.

❑ ❑ ❑

SECTION III

Official Occasions

Board of Directors' Meeting-I

(Speech by the Managing Director)

Mr Chairman and gentlemen!

At the outset, I may apprise you of the schedule of a very important agenda that today we have assembled here to discuss.

We have to decide two main points conclusively. The first point is the amalgamation of our company with our

competitor company and the second is the choice of management.

The indications are that our rival company is willing to merge with our company. If this happens, we will be controlling about 75 per cent of market and our separate advertisement costs as well as our competitive sales commissions will go down. This way, we'll be able to save on expenditure costs.

Secondly, though amalgamation will be a profitable proposition for both the companies, the question of management remains to be solved. We can decide by votes in Directors' meeting as to who or rather which company's official can be recommended for the top executive post in the merged company.

Alternatively, a rule can be framed that each company will have the top executive by turn, one after the other, year by year. This would appear to be a good arrangement. However, the only flaw in this arrangement is that the change of the top executive so often will not be a good prospect for the continuity of the company's policies and the management of its affairs.

Nonetheless, we must decide these issues today as day after tomorrow I will be meeting the managing director of the other company over lunch. The financial managers of both the companies will also be present with me.

Gentlemen, I invite your opinions about what interactions I should have with my counterpart. After we have talked things over in the preliminary round, we may hold a joint meeting of the Boards of Directors of both the companies.

We would meet again after lunch when I can have your opinions on these issues.

Thank you.

❑ ❑ ❑

Board of Directors' Meeting-II
(Speech by the Chairman of the Board)

Gentlemen!

This meeting has been convened to acquaint you with the fact that it has now become essential for us to diversify our activities to keep pace with the trade and commerce scenario of the country.

Your opinion is very essential as we have come to a point where the demand for our product has reached its saturation point. Besides us, all the firms making similar products are having their separate markets. We have now reached a status of equilibrium and without disturbing this equilibrium, we cannot increase or lose our sales.

The time has, therefore, come for us to diversify our business and take up another related product, the market for which is still expanding. A feasibility report shall be soon made available to you to help and decide on the issue which is based on a market survey conducted by our research and technical departments.

Once the issue of diversification is decided, then of course, it would be easier to take decision on various other issues such as fresh capital issue, factory expansion, accounting, advertisement and so on.

However, after the product is launched on a full scale, it is certain to have a successful launch in the market as a high demand product will be selected. Thus, we will have enough time before we may face big competition.

Thus, gentlemen, this is the meeting to apprise you of the outline of our next programme. You have enough time to deliberate on the matter. When the feasibility report is ready and by the time we meet again, we will have our fixed opinions on the subject.

Thank you for your cooperation.

❑ ❑ ❑

Delegation's Visit
(Speech by the Leader of Delegation)

Respected leader and the members of the host country (name of the host country) delegation, Excellencies, ladies and gentlemen!

It is a moment of great joy for me as I have come to your illustrious country. Also, it gives me an immense pleasure to lead my delegation to your country to further economic and industrial cooperation between the two countries.

As the world situation is changing very fast, it is important to strengthen bilateral ties because in the midst of chaos and confusion around us, these bonds and ties will help us grow and prosper.

Our two countries, both in political and economic fields, have parted with the traditional ways and values and have instituted the new and liberalised economic systems. These have opened up vast opportunities for cooperation between our countries and other nations of the world.

Your country has been doing very well in the economic front. Your GDP growth has been on a consistent rise for the last many years. Per capital income is also growing. It is worth appreciating that your country has achieved self-sufficiency in many sectors, notable among which is the agriculture and foodgrains sector. Your progress in the field of technological development has also been significant and of course, all these can be achieved by a well-managed and efficient mechanism of planning and execution.

Now, the time is ripe and opportune to build up financial and technical collaborations by way of joint ventures, scientific research, extension of tours and so on.

I am sure that our visit to your country will be very fruitful and there is great possibility that many proposals related to cooperation in different fields would emerge from this visit.

Thank you.

❑ ❑ ❑

Welcoming Delegation
(Speech by the Host Country's Delegation Leader)

Respected leader and members of the foreign country (name of the country), Excellencies, ladies and gentlemen!

It gives me great pleasure to welcome you to our country. I, on behalf of my country and my people extend to you, Mr Robins and all members of your delegation, a very hearty and cordial welcome to our country.

It would be our sincere efforts to make your stay in our country most memorable and comfortable. As you have mentioned Mr Leader that both the countries have lifted restrictions on trade, commerce and business ventures, there is a great possibility now for the two countries to explore and work out plans for suitable collaborations in various fields. Such collaborations can

be promoted between your country, our country and other countries of the world too. In the fast shrinking world of globalisation and liberalisation this is the best way for our growth and prosperity.

We have the technology and you have the resources and the process is complementary. Your resources can be blended with our technique, while our resources can be blended with those of yours. The results would be beneficial for both of us.

During the stay of your delegation in our country, we have arranged for you the visits to different areas such as those related to agriculture, industry and mining. We have arranged quite a few meetings with our entrepreneurs too so as to provide you an insight into the issues concerned.

We hope that all these efforts initiated by us will bear positive results.

Thank you.

❑ ❑ ❑

Felicitation
(Speech by the Sponsor)

Mr Chairman, Excellencies, ladies and gentlemen!

This meeting is being held to honour Dr Gordon Thomb who has been acclaimed as one of the best surgeons by the apex world bodies of medicine and surgery and who has been admitted to the prestigious Surgery Academy of international repute.

This is really a great honour for our country as one of our citizens has made his mark in the world forum of surgery and has pitted his skills against the best surgeon of the world. We are proud of him and wish him many more success in life.

We will endeavour to appeal to the government to grant Dr Thomb all the facilities and equipment so that

he can open his own highly sophisticated operating clinic in our country. This will not only promote and propagate Dr Thomb's surgical skills, but will also help to develop his kind of superior expertise in the country. At the same time the people of the country would have the availability of world-class medical facilities.

We, from our organisation, offer our humble contribution of Rs 1,00,000/- towards setting up of his clinic and fulfilment of his meritorious goal.

We hope that the people of the country will be benefited with his world-class skills, he would stay and work in his own country and bring further laurels to his people and country.

I would now request Dr Gordon Thomb to come on the stage and accept the cheque and the 'citation plaque' from the chairman. Ladies and gentlemen, please give him a big hand.

Thank you.

❑ ❑ ❑

Condolence Meeting

Mr Chairman, ladies and gentlemen!

I am unable to find words to condole the death of a great and devoted social worker of our State, nay of our land, as late Williams.

Ladies and gentlemen, Williams had always been a good friend of mine and I find no embarrassment in saying that my victory at the Council elections was to a great extent influenced by the fact that Williams was on my side.

He had endeared himself to the people of all classes and strata irrespective of caste, creed and community. He possessed a simple and honest nature. He had love for all and strong determination to fight against all odds. If

there had been shortage of funds for any social service—health training, adult education, environmental protection, cleaning up of any area—he would immediately set about to raise funds.

People trusted him and had firm faith in his capability to do the work and get the work done. We all lovingly called him 'Wily'. He always helped those whoever approached him. He was a sincere fellow, an aware citizen and above all a good human being. He always had the bright smile on his face for all of us. The more I speak about him, the more my heart pains. He was snatched away by the cruel hands of destiny from all of us at the young age of only 34. What cannot be cured must be endured. We will always treasure his memory and pray to the Almighty to rest his soul in peace.

On Receipt of Award
(Speech by the Awardee)

Mr Chairman, Authorities, members of the Literary Academy and friends!

I feel elated today as this literary award which has been conferred on me, is the height of my achievement, glory and good luck. This prestigious award is the coveted presentation that a writer aspires to receive during his life span.

I extend my heartiest thanks to the Academy Authorities who chose me for this award. I am also thankful to millions of my readers who have been instrumental in bringing about rewards and recognition to me. Of course, it is one of the greatest and happiest moments of my life. This honour strengthens my commitment to literary excellence

and I would be all the more sincere in my endeavour to contributing the rich and varied literature of our country.

However, my greatest acknowledgements go to my country, her people, her habitat, flora and fauna and the rich variety of our thoughts and living. In fact, I have drawn my literary materials from all these and I remain indebted to all such factors and sources from which I have been taking continuously and that shaped my thoughts. My only ambition is to stand by my country, and to enrich its heritage of rich culture and tradition through my writings.

I thank all of you.

❑ ❑ ❑

Inauguration of Cultural Meet
(Speech by the Inaugurating Official)

Mr Chairman, Excellencies, respected guests, ladies and gentlemen!

It gives me immense pleasure to be here today to inaugurate the week-long cultural meeting organised by the well-known cultural organisation—International Cultural Association.

Culture, which is the core and kernel of human existence, is the measuring yardstick of civilization. Culture requires time to grow, though wealth and prosperity can come and go even in a day. They are transient. But the culture and civilisation are long and lasting. They are the heritage of a country. They represent

the national identity. The cultural programme that starts this evening will provide vivid picture of the rich heritage of country and will continue for a week covering panorama of cultural activities such as dance, drama, songs, skits, music competitions, and picture and painting exhibition.

The prime objective of organising such a function is to generate an awareness towards one's cultural heritage and promote cultural sensitivity among the people, especially the younger generation. A person may have a poet or an artist hidden within him, waiting to be explored. He blossoms with the appreciation and encouragement of others in the society. A person may be a writer, a painter or a singer, but there may be nobody to appreciate his paintings, songs and writings.

Creating art and getting appreciation or absorbing the same, are the two sides of the same coin and both are complementary to each other.

I hope that you will enjoy the programmes that have been carefully organised for you. These will give the participants enough encouragement and provide the audience with a rich variety of entertainment. Your appreciation will go a long way in taking these budding artists to a higher level of performance and perfection.

Thank you.

❑ ❑ ❑

Inauguration of Trade Exhibition
(Speech by the Chairman of Trade Association)

Mr Chairman, Excellencies and dear exhibitors!

It is a moment of great joy for me to inaugurate this trade exhibition. I have been invited to declare this exhibition open to the public and to the business community.

We now live in an age which is moving very fast towards globalisation, liberalisation and free trade. Trade is a vital artery of the economic life of a country. There are many products produced by other countries that are required by us. Similarly, our country produces goods which are needed by other countries. Thus we are interdependent. We depend on other countries for some of our needs while we are suppliers of several requirements of many countries of the world. Thus trade is reciprocal. We import something from them and export many things

to them. This way we can save costs and have advantages of comparative costs.

Trade exhibitions are very important media through which we come to know about each others' products. They offer an opportunity to know and see the products developed by other countries. One speciality of the exhibition is that a 'special services' section is set up where the businessmen of different countries can see for themselves what specialised services are offered by an individual country.

There will be an exchange of views, opinions and expertise during the exhibitions. Also, we are expecting many business delegations from various countries to visit this exhibition. Such exhibitions greatly help in boosting trade and commerce among the countries and within the country itself.

I hope that many fruitful business deals will be signed before the exhibition ends in two weeks' time and there will be good business during the time. Hopefully, exhibition will serve its objective of expanding your knowledge in your respective fields.

Excellencies, honoured guests, ladies and gentlemen, I now declare this exhibition open to all and request our chief guest, the Honourable Minister of Commerce, to cut the ribbon at the entrance to inaugurate the exhibition formally.

Thank you.

❑ ❑ ❑

Function of Poor Relief Association
(Speech by the Chairman)

Gentlemen!

At the outset, I would like to greet you all and thank you all for attending this meeting of the Association. Our Association, Poor Relief Association, has completed five years and I feel proud to announce that during this span of time our Association has performed extremely well.

Our aim at the start of the Association was to provide relief to the poor of our area in the fields of health, education and employment. It was a humble beginning. Initially it was started at local level. However, our vision was to extend it to the whole of the state and then to the length and breadth of our country.

Our Association has been successful in achieving two

of our missions. Our workers are now engaged at the state level and our finances are now applied to this effect. We have expanded our activities to provide education and employment to all. Our Association has opened primary schools in remotely backward areas where there are no facilities to offer free education particularly to the poor children. We have also set up a training centre for women where women from all walks of life can learn various commercial arts and activities such as tailoring, cooking, food preservation, embroidery, etc. largely with an objective to make them economically independent. Recently, we have set up nursing homes in a few backward districts of the state so as to provide quality medical facilities to the poor and deprived section of society who do not have access to such facilities.

Hence it gives me an immense joy to preside over this annual function of the Association. The Secretary of the Association will later give you the details of the associated activities of the Association to apprise you of the patronage and assistance that we have been receiving from the state government and other organisations.

We have been receiving great help and assistance from big corporate houses. In fact, they are of tremendous help in our mission. One of our patrons will soon be sponsoring a charity cultural function to raise funds and to bring our Association to the limelight.

I hope that by next year's meeting our Association will have more members to help in realizing its noble cause.

Thank you.

❑ ❑ ❑

Shareholders' Meeting
(Speech by the Chairman)

Ladies and gentlemen!

I thank you all for coming here to attend this shareholders' meeting of our company. I also extend my thanks for your continued patronage and your trust reposed in the company's activities.

Ladies and gentlemen, this is your company and you have every right to know about what is happening in the company, what has been its performance during the last financial year and presently what is the financial status of this company.

I must assure you all that your company is doing consistently very well and there is no scope of worry from any quarter. Our production and sales have gone up. There is no doubt that competition is also catching up. However, we have made adequate provisions to take care

of this competition. We are continuously improving our products to deliver the best to our customers at most competitive prices. This is, in fact, the best thing which has helped the company to sustain its growth rate even in the face of stiff competition.

Besides, we have undertaken huge advertisement programmes through different media such as newspapers, radio and T.V. Also, we are exploring new markets to promote our exports and our products are being exhibited in many expositions and trade fairs outside our country as well as within our country.

Our products, as a result of all these promotional measures, have not only stood successfully against all competitions but are gaining good grounds in foreign countries. The rising demands of the products in the country and abroad have resulted in their growth. On the whole, the affairs of the company are being well looked after. The company has declared 15 percent dividend this year. This is a very good performance taking into consideration the fact that many companies have not declared any dividends at all at the end of the financial year.

Early next year, we would be having some rights issue and all you shareholders will get the chance to increase your equity holdings.

Ladies and gentlemen, I wish you all the best and expect that all your trust and confidence in the company will continue as ever.

Thank you.

❑ ❑ ❑

SECTION IV

Situations

Get-together
(Speech by the Host)

Friends, ladies and gentlemen!

We do not get the chance to meet very often like we have today. I am very happy to have you all at one place and at one time. We all have our engagements, different works to do and our preoccupations and yet we do meet

sometimes, as we need to relax and to get to know one another better. It is a great time for all of us because it offers us an opportunity to share our thoughts with one another.

It is primarily with this aim in view that I have invited you today. We are like-minded friends, who do not complain against one another, even though we have differences of opinion on some issues. We have great regard for one another and we also respect one another's views and opinions. In fact we enjoy one another's company. It is good to meet sometimes so that we can refresh ourselves by having small and big talks and laugh away our cares and worries with the help of others who are dear to us.

I hope you will enjoy this get-together and that tomorrow we shall have fresh energy to face the day.

Thank you friends and enjoy yourselves.

Cocktail Party
(Speech by the Guest)

Friends, ladies and gentlemen!

It is really a very pleasant evening and I heartily thank our host who has invited us all to enjoy the cocktail party.

We are sure to feel elated and in high spirits as we sit together and interact, as we enjoy the wine and liquor. On behalf of all of you I thank our host a second time for providing us with this moment of great ecstasy.

As we sip our drinks in this small gathering, many of the burdens, tensions and loads are lifted from our minds and we go back home in a light-hearted mood. I hope we will add our respective shares to build up this mood.

Thank you all and enjoy yourselves.

❑ ❑ ❑

Welfare Society
(Speech by the Chairperson)

Ladies and gentlemen!

You all know that the rights of women are clearly defined and laid down in the Constitution of India but they are not implemented in the right spirit. The reason is that the social upbringing of women keeps them quiet and prevents them from coming out in the open to denounce their tormentors or assert their rights. Our welfare society is for the uplift of the pressured and pressed women. It fights for those women who don't have means to fight for their own rights. In addition, it attempts to aware and educate women about their rights.

Our society is now moving forward. It is getting success in its mission. Women only can understand the misery of women. Therefore, as women's organisation, we have taken up the cudgel to strike at the roots of social

evils and social exploitation. In this struggle against the misdoings against women, we purport to educate women and make them independent. We provide them different kinds of training so as make them economically independent.

One of the causes of the upperhand wielded by those who mistreat women is women's dependence on others. We would like to have as much cooperation from the people as possible. If public opinion is adequately built up, persons who exploit the women will for fear of losing moral support of society, will not dare to commit crime against women. Thus mobilising public opinion against the crime against women will be of great help in this regard.

In this meeting, therefore, we would like to enroll volunteers—both male and female—who are eager to work against injustice to women in their area and also elsewhere. These volunteers will report the matter to us. We would endeavour to rectify the wrongs by peaceful means. However, if this approach fails, we would not hesitate to initiate stricter and stronger steps against the perpetrators of evil against women. The law is with us.

In most of the cases of ill-treatment against women, good advice and vigilance are enough to bring the culprits back to their senses. Thus, our main motto is to provide equal rights and full justice to women, in real sense, not only on papers. We attempt to ensure them a life of dignity and self-respect—a life, in which they have ample opportunity to grow and prosper. We are open to all your advice for the same. And look forward to your full cooperation.

Thank you.

❑ ❑ ❑

Post-dinner Speech by the Guest

Ladies and gentlemen!

At the outset, I extend my heartiest thanks to the host country for the warm welcome and hospitality that we have received here. Our programme and schedule were very meticulously drawn up, keeping in view the various sectors of economic activities that our delegation represents.

We have been able to meet our counterparts in your business fields with identical interests and I am sure that after both the sides discuss the opportunities in our respective countries, we would be able to finalise a number of deals.

As a leader of my delegation, I would like to extend an invitation to the representatives of your business

community and especially to the leader of your delegation to come to our country to initiate business venture so as to strengthen the bilateral economic ties and spurt the growth momentum of the country. I would like to add that our mission in your country has been quite satisfactory and successful for which we remain thankful and indebted to the authorities of your country and to all of you for the support and cooperation extended.

Thank you.

❑ ❑ ❑

Post-dinner Speech by the Host

Ladies and gentlemen!

This is the last dinner after our engagements, deliberations and interactions between the delegations of the two countries. The last three days were very hectic as we had a tight schedule of meetings and visits. I am sure that both the sides are quite satisfied with deliberations and discussions.

I am very thankful to the leader of the visiting delegation who has given us firm assurances that we may expect another business delegation from their country at the end of this year.

We would be very happy to receive such a delegation and we hope that this would mark the beginning of reciprocal visits to each other's country. Certainly, it would strengthen the bilateral ties between the two countries. Besides, it will boost the trade and commerce between them as well.

We look forward to having such prospects for which we extend our heartiest thanks. Here I conclude my speech and bid you farewell.

I wish you all a very happy journey.

❑ ❑ ❑

Club Meeting
(Speech by the Secretary)

Gentlemen!

This meeting of the Executive Committee of the club has been called to decide on a significant development about which there is no provision in the laid down rules of this club.

Gentlemen, it has been observed during the last few months that many members of the club have been bringing their guests with them. We were under the impression that the members of the club would bring mainly their relatives and immediate friends and thus keep the number of guests restricted. However, it appears that the members have not paid any heed to this point.

Our food and drinks are sold at concessional rates and it will not be possible for the club to accommodate so many guests.

I, being the Secretary of this club, is entrusted with the responsibility of ensuring the discipline and well-being of the club. I, therefore, propose that we should amend the guest rules of the club and keep the guests limited to immediate relatives—one or two in number at one time. If the members of the club agree to this amendment, we will proceed formally to do the needful. (All the members agree)

Now gentlemen, we call off this meeting and will meet very soon for the necessary action.

Thank you.

❑ ❑ ❑

Upliftment of Children

Mr Chairman, honourable chief guest, ladies and gentlemen!

I am happy to say a few words on the upliftment of children—a subject which is of vital importance to all of us, our society, our nation and our civilization as a whole.

Children are the future of the nation. They are the buds which must be allowed to bloom in full. When these buds—the future of our generation—bloom fully, they display their grandeur and spread their fragrance all around. Then the work of society is accomplished.

We must provide all facilities and opportunities to our children. It is the primary duty of every parents to provide nutrition, education and health care to the children. This is not only our duty but also the basic right of all the children. We have no right as parents to bring them into

this world if we cannot care for them and provide them the initial protection. By not doing so we will be exposing the children to the avoidable hardships and hazards of this world.

If we grow a small flower plant in our garden or in a vase, we have to water it regularly and take care of it in order to facilitate its unobstructed growth. A child is very much like a flower plant who needs to be tended and looked after. A child is dependent on the parents and guardians without whose care he is vulnerable to many risks and problems.

Small children are tender in feelings. They require and desire our attention and care. How vulnerable they are! There is no doubt that some children are destined to grow without being cared much. However, if not cared properly, the tender hearts of these children, their feelings and in fact, the sensitiveness of their minds would be checked, crushed and blunted.

There have been successful businessmen and other persons who rose to great heights though their childhood was spent in the worst frustration. The outcome of growth without care may have disastrous results for the society. Neglected and deprived children develop in them a universal antagonism against the entire humanity. Balanced growth of their personality is hampered. Memory of neglected childhood leads to the development of negative traits in them such as disregard for discipline, violent nature, etc. They may seek to destroy every good order and resort to evil thoughts and actions. Such children are sure to grow up to become anti-social elements and even criminals whose only aim of life may be to wreck the fabric of society. In fact they turn out to be a big challenge to society.

They are likely to become the dregs of the society—its unwanted, tarnished and abhored section. Who is to be blamed for? The blame surely falls on us who are the parents, the guardians or the society as a whole.

Ladies and gentlemen, these facts are not new and we all are aware of them. Idle deliberations and discussions will lead us nowhere. We should awake and act towards bringing out some change in our social system in which every child gets ample opportunity to grow. We should work for welfare of a child and we can pull a child out of dark and show him the path to light.

We must shake ourselves out of inertia and inaction and channelise all our efforts to productive work towards the welfare of the children. Every moment is precious. We can save the lives of unprivileged children of our land. India's unequivocal commitment to the cause of children, is well expressed in constitutional provisions, legislations, policies and programmes. The Directive Principles of State Policy and the Fundamental Rights clearly manifest this commitment of government towards the child welfare. In the framework of UN cooperation, the developed countries of the world are urged to contribute one per cent of their national income towards assisting the developing countries.

We can also initiate some such steps. Even a very small amount from each family—monthly or yearly—can make a large sum of money which can be utilised for the growth and career build-up of so many unprivileged children.

Many governments of the world are now aware of the great treasure that is confined in human resources and children constitute its significant part. Proper development and application of such resources and the judicious mobilisation of the same can provide the reservoir of man power which will contribute to the growth of a nation. Always remember "child is the father of the man".

Thank you.

❑ ❑ ❑

Banquet Toast

Mr Brennet, the leader of the International Car Association, Excellencies and honourable guests!

The illustrious Mr Brennet and his expert delegation have brought the message to promote close contact between their country and ours.

The two countries are now going to enter into an era of long-standing economic and business ties. We wish Mr Brennet and his delegation a very pleasant stay in our country and a safe and satisfied return to their country.

I propose a toast to the health and prosperity of the members of the delegation. I also propcse a toast to the bright future of the two countries.

To Mr Brennet and his delegation, gentlemen! (The host raises his glass of wine along with others and drinks from the glass.)

❑ ❑ ❑

Picnic Party

Friends!

I would like to say a few words before we actually begin the enjoyment of today's picnic.

As you all know that this picnic is not the yearly official picnic that we hold. In the annual picnic, all from the top executive of our office to the low-rung employees participate. Since the annual picnic becomes a little too formal and thus goes, in a way, against the spirit of the picnic atmosphere, we have planned this picnic.

This mid-year picnic has been arranged as an informal affair where all officers and subordinates can participate freely and thus derive pleasure from mixing together and from exchange of funs and thoughts.

In fact, we are not governed by etiquette in picnic and picnic time is the period when we have to forget ourselves and give ourselves to the friendly enjoyments. We are free to make fun and enjoyment. We should enjoy freely and expect others to do so. We should not hold ourselves back.

Let us enjoy today in the spirit of freedom of action, thought and speech. That is how we can make this picnic a success.

So friends, come and join the party. Let us fulfil ourselves in our picnicking. I welcome you all to this picnic party.

Thank You.

❑ ❑ ❑

SECTION V

Miscellaneous

Health Programme

(Speech by the Chief of the Health Association)

Mr Chairman, honourable chief guest, ladies and gentlemen!

There is a general saying that 'health is wealth'. If a person has a lot of money, and he suffers from ill health, mental depression and thus unable to lead a healthy life, then he cannot enjoy his money. One may have a

delicious spread of food on one's table, but if one does not have appetite or the capacity to digest it, that food is useless to him.

It is our duty to chalk out the best health programmes for the betterment of the society. We must make the health programmes most effective for the children. If we are able to make our children strong and can make them grow to their fullest, the children will be having a good start in their lives. Health has been at the centre of every welfare programme. It has been an area of prime concern for the government. Improvement in health and the nutritional status of the population holds great importance for a country.

Children are the future of the country. They are the asset to the nation. Thus, our programme on health should begin with children at home and at school. If children are healthy and strong, they can face various competitions and challenges of life with full confidence. Many affluent homes may be careless about a child's health requirements. The children should have balanced diet so that they get the proper amount of calories required for their growth and well-being. If the parents are aware of the health value of the different food items, whatever may be the food habits of the family, the children are given the right quantity of proteins, vitamins and other nutrients, etc. in their food they will grow into healthy citizens.

The tiger is a meat-eater. You may give it bucketfuls of meat but it will eat the quantity that is needed for one meal. Food is essential for sustaining life but the intake of the required quantity of food at different meals is very important. Unfortunately, this instinct of restraint in consuming food is found lacking in very few human beings. If a person knows when to stop, though he may have a spread of best dishes before him, most of his health-related problems will disappear. As we all know that overeating is one of the major causes of health related problems. Animals use this instinct correctly but many people while consuming food, use this instinct irrationally.

Coming back to children, the all-round development of a child depends on good health. If a child is physically strong and healthy, he will certainly have good mental health as a good mind is in a healthy body. Hence attention should be paid to the overall growth of children both at home and school.

The children health care programmes should be coordinated by the state authorities. Vaccines, injections, administration of pills and potions at proper times according to the age of a child should be arranged by the parents and school authorities so that the child grows up healthy. Also, the atmosphere at home and school should be hygienic with focus on sanitation and health care. This way not only the children but also all members of the family can lead a healthy and normal life.

However, a proper health programme by the government should include every citizen. No nation can be healthy and strong unless every segment of its society is strong. Health education and clean living habits are essential for every human being. The government must open information and treatment camps in different parts of the city so that the peoole are aware of the civic duties, health check-ups, etc. Besides, health awareness programme should be initiated so as to educate and aware people of the importance of health. Prevention is always better than cure. Ladies and gentlemen, I would like to conclude that this way all of us can lead a healthy, comfortable and prosperous life.

Thank you and have a healthy life ahead.

❑ ❑ ❑

Victory in Election

(Speech by the Elected Member)

Dear friends, brothers and sisters of the constituency!

Today is the happiest day of my life and it is also a day of rejoicing for all of us. In fact, the victory in the elections is not my victory but the victory of the righteousness; the truth has prevailed. Your wish has been granted and I have come out as a victorious candidate among the other contestants.

I fall short of words to thank you for your love, cooperation and above all confidence evinced in me. Your overwhelming support for me in the elections has made me speechless. I hope and do promise that I'll do my best to serve the people of this constituency. Development of my constituency will always find importance in my priority list.

You are all aware that I am just one arm and the government machinery has many such arms. However, I stand for you. I am fully aware of your problems, difficulties and demands—not really demands, but what you genuinely deserve. I can assure you that as your elected representative, I'll be your true representative before the government and that I will put your interests before the national body.

I will lend my ear to all your grievances and complaints. If I am not able to do so for sometime due to other pressing work, which may require my priority attention in the national interests, I will eagerly looking for time to sort out your problems. I will never shun my responsibilities and commitment made. I will never resort to deliberate indifference to your demands, requirements and genuine grievances.

I will very soon put into practice some measures which will enable you to have access to me anytime to communicate and interact with me. All of you are welcome to my office anyday, anytime. You can present your letter of complaint or whatever it is either directly to me or my competent staff. Also you can e-mail your grievances and complaints to my e-mail ID.

I assure you that all such letters will be processed and attended to without delay.

The job of bettering work lies before us and we have to do it on a cooperative scale. If I have your support, goodwill, trust and cooperation, I am sure, we'll be able to bring forth positive results in our administrative functioning which will lead to our prosperity and well-being.

You must have faith in me, your elected candidate, your rightful representative, for it is the biggest pillar of strength and manifest your patience and perseverance, to give me some time to enable me to set-up my office. Once everything gets in order, I will be taking up your cases before the judicial bodies.

I am aware that my constituency requires many civil and urban facilities such as better sanitation, better water-supply system, metalled roads and so on. Power supply is a big problem in the area. The situation gets worse during the summer where the gaps between demand and supply widen. Problem of frequent breakdown of communication network also calls for immediate attention.

I assure you that during my tenure, I will endeavour to upgrade all the facilities of this constituency and work for the upliftment of the masses.

I thank you once again.

Long live the country and long live the democracy.

Human Resources Development
(Speech by a Delegate at the Seminar)

Mr Chairman, honourable guests and Exellencies, ladies and gentlemen!

There is no denying the fact that in today's world, human being is going ahead with the help of technological developments and engineering know-how. Scientific research is to be co-opted in the developing system for quick progress and uplift of the living standards.

We have two alternatives in this context—either we leave human resources as they are and concentrate mainly on industrial development, or we motivate the growth of human resources simultaneously with industrial and technological development.

If the human resources are left on their own, there would be negligible improvements in these resources.

Also such improvements would not be according to any plan but susceptible to individual or group efforts. The outcome would be that some sections of the society would develop while some would remain underdeveloped. In the second alternative, human resources are given equal attention and importance along with economic development.

As a result, both human skills and efficiency, on one hand, and industrial and other developments on the other, move forward at the same pace.

The growth effect would be more spectacular, more effective and more disbursed among the whole populace in the planning system which gives us much predominance to the development of human resources as development in other spheres. The development of human race is key to the development of a nation. Human resources are valuable resources. Human resources are the backbone of a country. Even if a country is abundantly rich in natural resouces it cannot rise to height of great progress unless its human resources are developed.

Further, in the balanced growth of human resources, there will be less frustrations and less fears of failures. This will help in checking the growth and spread of crime. Therefore, there should be more co-operation and assistance from the people towards the success of planning.

All the countries are developing human resources. The underprivileged sections of society, the backward classes and those who are in the pits of hopelessness and misery, are to be brought up to the level of decency and normal living. They are to be educated and imparted the necessary skills so that they can earn their own living and be self-suffcient. Properly trained and highly skilled human resources are perceived as the greatest asset of an organisation. Skilled personnel contribute to efficiency, growth, increased production and improved quality of a product in an organisation.

The gap between the privileged and the non-privileged widens where human resources are not given proper opportunities for development and fulfilment of their aims. This breeds discontent and dissension. The social fabric runs the risk of getting pierced and torn to pieces, the balance of society is disrupted and social evils may spread to strike at the roots of settled establishments.

In short, not only should there be plentifulness of material goods, but also there should be development of human standards. There is better distribution of wealth and opportunity and there is higher stratum of human satisfaction under this dual advancement.

We should not be concerned only with material acquirements but also with the quality of life. The material wealth is best utilised and enjoyed when it is used to further the interests of culture, art, literature and enrichment of human mind. The developed mind can visualise an adorable and enjoyful future and we should work for such a schedule.

Thank you.

❑ ❑ ❑

Economic Planning
(Speech by the Chairman)

Honourable guests, ladies and gentlemen!

Planning plays a very important role in our lives, whether we plan for small things at home or whether there is a plan being drawn for the affairs of a country.

Upon getting up in the morning, we find that we have to do so many things in that single day. Obviously, we feel worried with the whole burden of the work and are at a loss to know what should be done first and what be done later.

In such circumstances, we should prioritise our tasks. The most important work must be done first, followed by the next important work and so on. If we follow this approach to complete the work, we can feel relaxed and

the stress will be automatically lifted from our minds. Besides, our work will also be completed in time.

This simple procedure should be adhered to while carrying out the economic planning of the country. If the priority is education, the government should gear up the machinery for the promotion of education. If agriculture or industrial development is to be assigned top priority, the main efforts should be guided towards that direction.

Proper planning, however, should not neglect the other sectors which are outside the priority area. All sectors in the country such as industry, agriculture, foreign trade, financial sector, transport and communications, tourism, child and women sector, youth and so on—should be made to grow. The country's funds and revenues should be adequately allotted to every sector so that all-round development takes place with special emphasis on the particular priority field.

Planning is important not only for the growth of the nation but also for individual careers. A plan is successful only when it is executed well in time. A plan has to reach its zenith of performance after it is started and also it should prepare the ground for the next planning session.

If one plan succeeds, we have a better beginning, and a higher level of starting for the next plan. Therefore proper planning would enable the country to move towards propserity in all directions.

As we are all aware, planning has to be within the framework of resources and with reference to specific targets to be achieved. The plan should have provisions for exigencies and emergencies that may occur to inflict setbacks to the plan, as there may be a difference in what we aim at—that is the visualised target and what we achieve in reality.

There can be natural calamities such as floods, epidemics, earthquakes, droughts, etc. Also, there can be international deterrents like wars, blockades, sanctions, financial crisis, etc. which can impede or harm the external sectors of economy like tourism, exports, imports, etc.

These impediments can be faced or tackled without much hindrance to the overall progress of the country if the plan has adequate provisions for these contingencies. These adverse events can be laid down as setbacks. These setbacks or reverses can delay the planning process or the expected results. However, if working mechanism is good, the country's economy can tide over these problems and continue to work in the direction of the achievement of its goals.

It is important to have a plan period. If a plan is drawn for a very long period, say ten to fifteen years, it will be difficult to keep track of the short-term and long-term results. On the other hand, If the plan is made for a very short time, then also the effects may not be correctly assessed, as there will not be the correct assessment of the links between investments and outputs.

It appears that the countries that had devised flexible plans, have benefited greatly from planning. The execution of the plan are calculated year by year and assessed against the targets in context of the new situations, new considerations and workouts are made to meet the challenges of the emerging situation.

The main emphasis of my speech is that if the plan

is disrupted and if it fails to achieve its desired targets and its expected results, even then it is better to be guided by an economic plan of revenues and receipts against expenditure. Without a proper plan, it is undesirable to carry on with the affairs of the state.

Thank you.

❑ ❑ ❑

Banking Development
(Speech by an Official)

Mr Chairman, respected chief guest, ladies and gentlemen!

As our civilisation advanced and people became more up-to-date in modern living, banking became a part and parcel of our lives. In fact, banking is the main artery of commercial life. The banking system has advanced very well in the developed countries. However, banking has undergone sea change in recent times in terms of quality of services and expansion of banking network.

The expansion of the banking system among the people, especially the rural population should be regarded as a big achievement. This marks the popularity of the bank particularly in rural areas. Not only do the extension

and acceptance of the banking habits prove to be favourable for the banking business, but they also mean more transactions with banks.

Such contacts will ultimately make the people realise about various opportunities that lie with the banking sector for the different sections of society.

As we are all aware, this is only one side of banking activities. Banks and the business sector are closely related to one another. We can't think of business without banks. The relationship between the banks and the commercial activities play a significant role in the growth of the country and the banking sector as well. In today's progressive process, credit is a very important phenomenon. The banks can have bigger and bigger deposits but this situation can hardly mean anything. For the banks, it is the efficient management of this credit which decides the growth of banks for this deposit is not for free but the banks have to pay interest on it.

The banks, therefore, lend a major part of this deposit to businessmen at higher rates of interest and the difference is, of course, to be regarded as the profits of the banks. If the lending by the banks is fruitful then only can the banks earn higher interest and grow at large.

If the banks can assist and back industries and business ventures which are profit-making and are capable of yielding better returns, the banks can go on having their higher interest at the same time the business units backed by them will also prosper.

Sometimes a bank has to select business activities for a credit. Some units may be starting at the scratch but the nature of the business may have good prospects and also the few transactions already completed may give promise of development.

There is no doubt that the bank which is forwarding the loan, has to take risk. However, 'risk' is the watchword of the business world. Besides, in the shrewdness of selecting good and prospective ventures, the bank authority's vision, right decision and correct knowledge would play a great part.

Thus, the banker, by his right decision can earn good profits for his organisation as well as he can give the necessary assistance to the business venture. This reflects the social concerns of the banking sector. It is one of the reasons behind the rising popularity of banking in India. If the businessman and his business are genuine and if the bank can help him at the time of initial financial troubles when his goodwill is not built up, the bank will really be doing a great service to the nation and to the national economy by helping the businessman get over his initial problems and sail smoothly in the world of business.

Therefore, banking development would depend on two factors—on the bank manager's correct foresight as to whom to lend and whom not to; secondly, in the context of the national business panorama, he has to set his priorities rightly.

Just as the individual branches have to be concerned with their revenues and expenditure and with the increase in their deposits range by expanding their customer-range, similarly, the central authorities of the banks have to draw up their plans and programmes for expansion of banking activities in the countries.

These plans refer to opening up of branches in new areas particularly in the remote parts of the country.

Besides, more and more ATMs need to be installed particularly in remotely backward areas. Moreover, banking procedures should be simplified so that a common man can avail the facilities extended by banks. The banks should be friendly and transparent in their dealings and customer satisfaction should be the watchword of the whole banking business. With this, business activities will get boost throughout the length and breadth of the country, leading to the growth of the economy as well.

Banking is a boon to the financial world and let us share this boon.

Thank you.

Environment and Mankind
(Speech by an International Expert)

Ladies and gentlemen!

At the outset, I would like to thank the sponsors of this meeting under whose aegis I have got this opportunity to interact with you.

Today, environment is not an isolated subject that can be discussed or studied as something of academic interest. However, environment is initimately woven into the fabric of human existence and is thus a very much topical issue. In fact, it is a major issue and one of the most discussed topics.

To begin with, we have to go back to the beginning of history to identify environment with nature as well as the life and habits of human and other beings. There is environment of the seaside, of the mountains, of the desert region; there is environment of the cold countries and the environment of hot and humid atmosphere.

Also, we have the forests, the water sheds, the greenery and so on. We fell trees and sell out the logs. We reclaim the waterways for building homes and blast the mountains to expand our rural or urban civilisation. We clear forests to set up factories or make our dwellings. However, we don't realise that these actions of man are hazardous for human existence. By doing so we disturb both flora and fauna.

When the trees are felled and the mountain slopes are bared off the greenery, we, in fact, cut off a part of nature that existed to supply man with the nourishment of clearner and purer atmosphere. The chimney smoke from our factories and the gases emitted by vehicles and the chemical wastes flowing into our rivers, pollute the air we breathe in and the water we consume.

Apart from this, the fish and other acquatic animals which are good source of nourishment to some sections of mankind, become tainted due to water pollution and become unfit for consumption. Polluted water also damages the acquatic vegetation. Thus, man is proving to be his own enemy by disturbing nature and polluting the very surroundings of human existence. His activities are degrading environment. In big cities and towns population is increasing and natural resources are indiscriminately being exploited to provide for the basic requirements of the population. There are no proper arrangement for waste disposal. Besides, the use of insecticides and pesticides in our farm is also a big source of pollution. The increasing number of vehicles is making the air dirty. Many maladies can be avoided if we are able to breathe fresh air.

By holding meetings and discussions on environment, the task does not become easy. People have to cooperate with the authorities. People must cooperate in implementing the rules enacted by the government. Unless people are well aware of their duties and responsibilities, we cannot save our environment. Government can enact laws, but it is up to us to abide by the rules and regulations. So we should cooperate with the government which is important for the larger interest of mankind.

It is not only through regulations that we can save our environment but also through realisation that man and nature can co-exist in complete peace. Environment preservation is sometimes a high-sounding word but at times it becomes a way of life with the people.

It is the responsibility of every citizen to keep our environment clean and healthy. Children should be taught from their tender age that maintaining the natural existence and beauty is an important aspect of life. It is the duty of all men, women and children to enrich nature and the natural environment by their daily deeds, by keeping their surroundings and their habitation clean and hygienic for their own good.

Thank you.

❑ ❑ ❑

Conference on Human Rights
(Speech by a Delegate)

Mr Chairman, fellow delegates, ladies and gentlemen!

Among all other kinds of living things man has risen to be the supreme being. Man has been able to achieve this height through the application of his rationality. His spirit of cooperation and help are the other qualities and attributes that have helped man to move ahead of other animals.

But, the towering ambition of man keeps on moving upward and in his flying-high spree, man tends to be blind to the needs and requirements of all around him. In order to have more and more, he only follows the urge to reach his goal. In pursuit of this goals, he sometimes becomes quite insensitive towards other fellow being. He has his target and he wants to achieve it anyhow.

All human beings are ambitious to a certain degree, as ambition has its positive traits. Without having any ambition in life man would be like a ship without a rudder. As human beings, our feelings and understanding are our main assets. If in the course of our onward rush for success, we forget the noble qualities which God has endowed us with, if we are indifferent and insensitive to the welfare and well-being of others who are our fellowmen, we will definitely be doing injustice to the society. Hence, it will be something like trampling on the rights of other fellow human beings.

There is no harm in thinking about our betterment. However, we have no right to violate others' rights and discard their needs. Had we not to hold this conference on human rights, this world of ours would have been more beautiful and humane. Human rights would have been automatically respected and preserved and no deliberations would have been needed for their preservation.

It is unfortunate that such a conference has to be convened to create an awareness among the masses to uphold the individual's rights. It is unfortunate because we are selfish enough to overlook the interests of others. The issues relating to human rights' violations not only pertain to humans in general but also specific vulnerable sections like women, children, bonded labours, persons with disability and refugees.

If we view from the other angle, a conference of this nature and style manifests that we have not lost our balance in the zeal of our own improvement, that we are still sane enough to distinguish between the privileged and the non-privileged, the so-called haves and have-nots. It may be regarded as an achievement for us to acknowledge that we are so sensitive towards the rights and privileges of our fellow human beings that we assemble time to time, as we have done today, to survey the whole range of rights that our fellow citiizens are entitled to, but are deprived of the same.

There are now national and international human rights commissions, apart from various non-governmental organisations (NGOs), human rights/social activists which are vigilant to take up and investigate issues related to violation of human rights at national and international level.

However, it is quite true that despite well organised mechanism to check the violation of human rights, incidents of human rights violation are frequent and on the rise. It would not be wrong to say that such news has become a regular feature of media. Sometimes there are reports on custodial deaths and suicides in jail, often the news of the murder of someone in the name of caste and community becomes the headline. We come to know about people who are compelled to leave their homes because of militant and terrorist activities. Some persons are persecuted in their own countries and seek asylum or protection in another country.

Also, there are minorities who in some countries are not treated at par with the mainstream population. Though our deliberations might not legally achieve much in all countries, yet public opinion is a strong force. When truth of bad happenings is not suppressed and is allowed to come out publicly, our mission is achieved.

That the governments of the world have lent their allegiance to our organisation or other organisations, proves the goodwill shown by all nations and also it proves the point that in a world burdened with controversies, hope and human happiness can still thrive.

Thank you.

Long live humanity!

❑ ❑ ❑

Political Party's Annual Conference
(Speech by a Party Speaker)

Mr President, party colleagues and honourable guests!

The point of time at which we have gathered here is very important for all of us, as the general elections are round the corner. This opportunity, therefore, for us is to review our performance and deliberate on our future prospects.

Many opposition parties have done better in elections of state assemblies since the last general elections. Our party leaders were more concerned about matters such as security as well as preventive measures against terrorism and communal dissentions within the country. Our efforts at national integration continued unabated and

our National Human Rights Commission has been doing a meritorious work since its inception.

Our external policies and political and economic administrations have been quite laudable. The management of our economy has been appreciated even by foreign governments and institutions. There is no doubt that democratic process has been established firmly.

Although everything is going on well and as per schedule, we have faced reversals in the assembly elections in some states. After analysing the causes, we have concluded that such reversals are but the natural fallouts of people's inclinations and desires for a change. People want a change hoping that a change would make them happier and prosperous.

This thinking of people is imaginary because economically and politically the steps initiated by us have been lauded by people in all walks of life. We have achieved maximum results in all sectors. Our granaries are full, exports are booming. Services sector is growing. Foreign investors and businessmen are having better confidence in our system and our native companies are spreading in other countries to get firmer footholds.

Middle class population is enjoying a much better status and having good opportunity to grow and prosper. The wages of labourers are increasing. Percentage of people living below poverty line is consistently declining. However, our political leaders are engaged more in other preoccupations. As a result, they have less time to establish, renew and strengthen their contacts and interactions with the common man. Such people have nowhere to take their grievances to except to somebody who can lend them ears.

We should never regard this as a useless work because our destiny is in the hands of the people who have voted us to power. It is the power of the masses which facilitate our march through the gallery of power. However, we have every hope that after assessing our performance people will stand by us with their full support and confidence in us despite any publicity or propaganda against us.

However, it is time now that we should—everyone of our party—find time to be with the people to explain to them that real progresss does not exist in populist measures—giving them subsidies, pensions, free food and lodging but to take the country's growth to such a height that each citizen, each individual finds opportunity to grow and earn enough to fulfil his bare minimum needs.

We must convince the people that the real assistance is to make the people self-reliant and self-sufficient so that they earn more and more and contribute to the country's development in a much bigger way and that aiding the people with subsidies and concessions can be regarded as a wrong approach to development of society.

Thank you.

National Seminar on the Role of Teachers

Honourable chief guest, ladies and gentlemen!

I regard teachers as the most important members of the society and hence I feel immense pleasure to address you today. I have always had a great respect for the teachers right from my childhood.

Our civilization rests completely on teachers and, in fact, they are the builders of our community, society and nations. It is the teachers who guide and shape the career of a student who is the leader of tomorrow. If the students are inculcated with good moral values and imparted good education, the future of the country is bound to be good. The students of today will imbibe and propagate the civilization of tomorrow.

Once a film actress was asked a question as to what she thought about teachers and her reply was that she considered teachers to be the most perfect of beings. She was, no doubt, right. The students who are being taught consider their teachers as the be-all and end-all of superiority. I would like to illustrate an incident which is relevant in this context.

I know the head of our coaching institute who would get lots of school dropouts and rowdy students of very low intellectual levels. These students would get coaching in this institute to appear as private candidates in school final examinations. Before selecting a teacher, he would put him provisionally in the most indisciplined class. If the teacher was able to manage that class, could keep the class quiet, then he was selected and no other recommendations were required.

You all teachers should keep this in mind that if a teacher is good in his or her field of teaching, if the teacher loves the students and is committed to his profession, he would be doing his duty in the best manner.

I think as teachers we must remember that students are not our competitors, they are our wards. There is no good student or bad student but just 'student' who, of course, may have his or her limitation of intelligence, his capacity to understand and assimilate. A committed teacher grooms his intellect and helps him develop his personality.

Parents and teachers are the two pillars of a child's citadel. The structure of the child's career and life rests on these two pillars. If parents on one hand and the teachers on the other, guide the child in the right direction, there is every certainty that the child would bloom to the best according to his inherent talent.

Ladies and gentlemen, teaching is one of the noblest professions and a sacrificing one too. It is sacrificing because the students learn not only from the words of the teachers but also from the life and code of conduct followed by the teachers. Hence, teaching is a very responsible job.

I hope all the teachers will realise their true responsibilities and remain sincere and committed to their profession.

Thank you.

❑ ❑ ❑

Business Meeting

Mr Chairman, the honourable chief guest, ladies and gentlemen!

We have assembled here to take very important decisions on quite a few important issues. When a person or a group starts a business, it may be started in isolation. However, soon the complex nature of the business world catches up with the working of the business unit. The unit has to face national and global competition and also many regulations, strictures and a number of situations—some of which may be favourable and some not so favourable.

At the very outset, we must realise that an industrial or business venture is not simply an individual or sectional affair. But it is a national and global affair and hence a venture of this kind requires cooperation of all the

people—the government as well as the foreign investors. A successful national expertise benefits foreign investors also, as they can have the chance to utilize transfer of technology from both sides.

A business enterprise has to thrive on the basis of community welfare. Whether we produce goods or services, the quality of our production should be the best. Cosumer satisfaction is of paramount importance for a business to grow. Besides, maximum public welfare should be the objective of such an enterprise.

Gentlemen, we cannot reap and keep our profits like that of a run-away fugitive. We have to live and work in society, we have to ensure the masses of our utility and we have to disburse this utility in an equitable manner among our fellow citizens. In fact, the benefits of this utility should percolate to the lower strata of society. Our norm should always be high, our target benevolent and our working should be above board. The business has to build up goodwill, prove its performance, sincerity and steadiness. There is no 'touch and go' in business. Sustainable growth in business can be maintained only by focusing on quality and customer satisfaction.

Just as we are committed to our business, we must be dedicated towards our objectives. Also, the country and the government have to cooperate with us to provide a boost to our objectives and push us in both national and international levels.

As we are national units we do not want that the government should help us blindly. However, some sort of security cover is required against those who may sometimes, seek to harm our growth through their unscrupulous deeds. Also, we should depend on our own people, our own nation to stand by us and promote and patronise our products and services.

This love for the goods of one's own country may be termed as true nationalism. Thus, every businessman should bank upon the support of his countrymen. When there is an irrational craze for foreign goods, and total rejection of anything produced nationally, irrespective of its quality and utility, businessmen are at a loss to fight a proclivity which is nothing but sort of an addiction. Hence the business community should be quite aware of the needs and choices of its own people so as to keep them attached with its products or services.

We are sure that our countrymen will extend their support and help us in launching our own business activities. Also, government would extend its all possible help to make our business, our venture stand against national and foreign competition.

We need not fear national competition if it is carried on in free and fair terms. In fact, healthy competition is necessary for a good business environment. The same contentions hold good about international competition also. However, if that competition is made unfair through protective duties abroad, or exports from abroad as 'dumping', then we should expect our government to help us through duty exemptions, etc. We should be allowed to prosper so that we can contribute our share towards national development.

Thank you.

❑ ❑ ❑

Science and Development

Mr Chairman, honourable chief guest, ladies and gentlemen!

We live in an age of scientific and technological development. In this age one who does not keep pace with scientific development will be left behind. One has to always keep pace with the new means of advancement in order to progress in one's field of activity.

In this race for going ahead, modern technology is the most useful tool which we can use to make our forward journey smooth and impressive. However, technology has the tendency to become obsolete. Everyday we have new technology, which is more upgraded and advanced than the previous one.

A gadget or equipment which is new today may become old tomorrow.

In order to protect us from such a pitfall, we have to adapt and adjust ourselves with new technology. Each new technology is expected to improve efficiency, reduce cost and save operational time and energy.

We have to harness the means supplied by science to our respective usefulness. In order to apply scientific methods in our lives to make our progress more successful, we should promote research and development. For this, we must have more and more research and development (R and D) organisations. Now, R and D is an integral part of our industrial network. Many industries have their own research and development units which continuously work for their own improvement in quality and cost.

Science is a vast domain of knowledge of nature's mysteries which would never exhaust and man can forever explore to find new methods of better living. Thus, science and technology have to run simultaneously.

New theories can be invented, new formulas drawn up, new medicines, new sources of energy, production, transportation, communication, etc. can lead man to enjoy life in a much better way.

Technology can be bettered through research and improvements in the ongoing processes. As technology is made superior, efficiency increases and the quality and standard of living improves. Science and technology are supplementary to each other. We cannot isolate one from other. Scientific inventions and innovations are necessary for the advancement of technology. At the same time, as the need for higher and sophisticated technology is felt, man engages himself more and more to scientific inventions which would give newer bases for superior technology. Therefore, one of the motivations behind scientific research is technology demand.

Progress has become the pastime in the modern age, so much so that old models of cars, machinery and equipment are discarded like old clothes. In consumer durables and goods like television sets, music systems, communication modes, refrigerators, electronics goods, the world is moving so fast that there is no time to stand and think.

Designers, scientists and manufacturers, in fact, everyone connected with the consumer products, is on a mad race, to reach the goal of maximum efficiency first.

Science has become the mainstay of our existence as scientific knowledge and development are now equal partners.

In this scenario, we should guide our children towards the development of scientific bent. They should be inculcated to have inquisitive and innovative minds from an early age.

We must remember that we have to keep pace with the progress and developments in the fields of science and technology.

Thank you.

Lawyers' Convention
(Speech by the Chief Guest)

Mr President, ladies and gentlemen!

It gives me immense pleasure to speak to you at this convention today. We all are aware of the fact that practising law is regarded as an honourable profession. Also, the esteemed audience knows well that the lawyer's is a dedicated and committed life.

The selfless service a lawyer gives to the society and his country, may or may not be compensated by the monetary consideration that he gets in return. However, the qualitative aspect of a lawyer's work deserves to be appreciated from all quarters. The lawyer, being a very important member of the community, stands between the law and the people, as well as between the law and the authorities. He serves as a link between the two.

A lawyer is there amongst us for the interpretation of the law of the land. Without the lawyer, the whole legal system, the gamut of rules and regulations and official acts and decrees, would remain lopsided or one-sided. It is also possible that in the urge and zeal to implement the tenets of codified regulations, there could be indiscriminate and unrestricted application of rules. The lawyers act as a break and provide yeoman service to the people and to the country by the exposition of rules and they also ensure how far these are to be made effective on the violators of the law.

Any person who is accussed of an offence may not be actually guilty unless his guilt is proved in the court of law. It is the lawyer who assists the judge in arriving at the right decision as to whether an offence or crime has actually been committed or not. Hence, in the lawyer's hands lies the success of democracy, for when two lawyers argue the case, for and against from positive and negative sides, a greater clarification of the issue or dispute comes to light and the judge and the jury may arrive at the truth behind the apparently wrong action. Therefore, if democracy in a country is to survive, if the rights of the individuals are to be upheld, the rightful participation of the lawyers in the legal system is very essential.

It is the duty of lawyers to explain to the judiciary and to the people the various details, degrees and nuances of the codified law. They expose some hidden facts and bring them to the notice of the judiciary. The lawyers also do a great service to the people and to the government by finding out the flaws, the loopholes, if any, in their efforts to save the clients.

It is through the arguments of the lawyers that the government realises and finds out the chinks and way-outs in an Act of the state, which have to be plugged and cemented. Through the subsequent amendments of the concerned Act, the government takes such measures. Thus, the services of the lawyers in a state are commendable from the point of view of security and general well-being. Gentlemen, my only submission to you is that considering the great trust and responsibility reposed in lawyers, the great social service the lawyers render to society and much needed academic interest they bring to the legal system, the lawyers are held in high esteem both by the state and the society.

However, there is no denying the fact that no light is without darkness, no rightful action is rightful without wrongful inclination and so on. This is only to indicate that since the lawyers are deeply involved in the legal system, explanations, etc. they can have in their hands the power of reflecting and interpreting the laws; and hence it is required of them to adhere strictly to the business ethics. Their attempt should be to expose truth and do justice with the victim. They should not be swayed by the material benefits.

It was Gandhiji who while practising as a lawyer, a long time ago, discovered the true duty of a lawyer. A lawyer, according to Mahatma Gandhi, should try to bring the two rival parties in case, to reconcile with each other without going into litigation. This way, much wastage of time and unnecessary expenses can be saved.

A real lawyer would fight a case more as a challenge than the academic interpretation of the law. Further, he would be more concerned about guarding the interests of his clients against all odds. Sometimes, clients come to a lawyer in a state of utter desperation and in such frustrated and helpless condition, the lawyer is their only beacon light. I hope all members of the legal profession, while dealing with their clients, will remember this fact. It is their responsibility to uphold the nobility of their profession, by doing justice with the victim and bringing the culprit behind the bar.

Thank you.

❑ ❑ ❑

National Students' Union
(Speech by the Student Leader)

Mr Chairman Sir, Minister of Labour, respected guests and friends!

It is a memorable occasion to address this annual event of students' unions of all institutions of the country. It is more an academic ceremony that brings the students from the different parts of the country on a single platform.

This platform offers an opportunity to those participants who wish to share their targets, and achievements, their ambitions and aspirations and also their problems and tribulations.

Friends, as you all are aware that youth is the prime stage of life, when one is full of energy and enthusiasm. He has vision, high ambition and energy to realise his dreams and ambitions. Hence it is incumbent on all of us—the students of this country—to talk less and work more. We should always attempt to do some constructive work in the larger interest of society. Before us lies the vast volume of work and we have to forge unity in the midst of diversities of ways, habits, customs and traditions.

Besides, each of us in his/her own way try to mobilize student power for the betterment of the country so that the basis of national unity becomes firmly rooted in our minds. Youth is an impressionable age—it is the age of work and progress. Lessons learnt during this age continue to guide throughout the life.

In all our diversions we should not forget our priorities and certainly our first priority is to progress in learning. We should be very sincere and focused to our tasks. We should always try to excel in our studies. Our parents, guardians and well-wishers have great expectations from us. They want to see us at the height of excellence. We only fulfil our primary objective when we fulfil their expectations. My message to all my fellow students is to ensure that on no account should we ever forget our goal of acquiring academic excellence and knowledge. That is the objective for which those who have sponsored us are making sacrifices. It is their dream that we prove ourselves worthy of their ideal and establish ourselves in our lives as responsible citizens.

If we think of this noble ideal of our parents and their simple aim of seeing us settled in life, it will pain us to see their ambition not fructifying if we indulge ourselves in careless ways. Therefore, on this day, we should take the vow that come what may, in order to crown us with glory in our student life, we will not veer from our primary objective of excelling in studies and put in all our efforts to fulfil the expectations of our parents.

We all are familiar with the adage that 'all work and no play, makes Jack a dull boy'. The message is clear in it. We should not confined ourselves to studies only. We have to be conscious about the world around us. We should not shut our eyes to our surroundings—to the happenings, the laws of the land and our people. We are the privileged ones as we are receiving education which many boys and girls of our age are deprived of. Hence we have the responsibility towards our society too.

Therefore, it is also our duty and one of the main responsibilities that we understand our country, its people and their problems. We should try to mark out the problems, needs and anguishes of other people so that when we get an opportunity in our life, we can try to eliminate the sorrows and sufferings of such people and lead our countrymen towards a more peaceful existence. However, that will be possible only when we acquire knowledge and capability to help them relieve of their sufferings. And of course, it is the acquisition of knowledge, and development of skills which will provide us opportunity to guide the destiny of our nation. However, before that opportunity comes there are many tasks which we can successfully accomplish without neglecting our studies and without becoming oblivious to our primary objectives.

To begin with, we must use our spare time in selfless work. We must devote our time in doing some social work. The student community can help and educate the common masses who do not know how to read and write. Sanitation, environment cleaning, adult education and even assistance in natural calamities like earthquakes and floods should be taken up by the students community on voluntary basis. We can go to the rural areas of the country and educate people about the modern and scientific ways of living thereby helping the villagers in leading lives free from disease. We should be aware of keeping our environment clean and green.

We should try to get ourselves acquainted with current political, economic and scientific and technological developments. Acquiring knowledge in these areas will supplement our theoretical knowledge which can prepare the base for our future career. Apart from all this, a student should take interest and participate in games and sports. These extra-curricular activities should be an integral part of our lives.

Students should also participate in dramatics, music, debates and other institutional activities which would provide us some relief from the pressure of studies and enrich our mental capabilities. Involvement in all these activities, however, should be on a balanced scale and never at the cost of studies.

We should not step off from the middle path which will lead us towards our educational achievements. Along with studies, we should study the pros and cons of our existing system and should be aware of plugging in the loopholes, wherever they exist. Thus, we should never be indifferent to our country's civilization and progress.

Dear students, we should be cautious about certain negative and unproductive aspects of our activities. We should guard ourselves against laziness, lethargy, lack of spirit of competition, addiction to anything, idle gossipping and unwanted ego. They have great negative impact on the development of our personality.

By adhering to these guidelines we can make our lives purposeful and also contribute our share to the national development.

Thank you.

❑ ❑ ❑

Violence Against Women

Mr Chairman, ladies and gentlemen!

It is a great honour to me to have been given an opportunity to express my views on a matter—that is one of the greatest social evils of our society—'violence against women'.

Women constitute half of the population. They are the producer of mankind. We cannot imagine a society without women. We should feel much pain and agony when we hear about any atrocity done to any woman.

When we think of a woman as a mother, a woman of any country, of any religion, caste, creed or status, our heads must bow down with respect. A mother has the feelings of love, care, sympathy and understanding for her offspring. For a mother, a child is never big enough. Whether a child is small, young, grown-up or aged, the

mother's love flows to him with equal intensity. Age makes no difference to her love towards her children. Therefore it is our duty to place our mother above everything else in our worldly consideration.

A mother may not ask much from her son or daughter or even she may ask nothing from her grown-up children. She may not have any expectation from the children. However, it is our duty that we must care for her, provide for her all the cares and comforts and show our respect to her.

Mother, sister, wife and daughter—the four faces, the four images of a woman are the most precious images. If any of us distorts or destroys any of these images, we cannot be called human beings but animals—nay, worse than animals because even animals have their natural code of conduct.

Woman is endowed with wonderful attributes and qualities. She has made great sacrifices for man as history and legends would show. With no concern for her own self, woman has made great sacrifices to save man.

A woman's sensitivity, by all means, would revolve round love for her beloved. In this feeling or relationship with man—with her beloved, she has practically very little thought for anything else except expectation of care, concern and love from the person she loves. Thus, she delivers maximum joy to her beloved. If a woman, the so-called weaker sex, with higher feelings and capacity to adorn this world with beauty, is ill-treated, it is a great shame for mankind. It is a shame for all of us—the mankind, notwithstanding the fact that the actual perpetrators of such a violence against the women may be someone else.

A sin committed by any male member of society against a woman is a slur on all the male members of the society. The males have proved to be a failure in protecting the women's rights in society.

There is no doubt that the root cause of this malady—the crime against women—lies in the crooked psychology of the concerned criminals. To rectify such criminals is not the subject of our discussion today. That may be left to social workers, medical practitioners and state authorities.

However, what is of significance to us is that if reason does not prevail, if culture, understanding, training and judgement fail, we have only one course left with us. Fear therapy should be made operative and such a fear can be evoked through stringent punishments. To say, those involved in crime against women should be dealt with hard-handedly.

The criminals who cannot be caught and go scot free, are, of course, out of our purview but those who are apprehended and whose guilt is proved, should be given the severest punishment.

I also cannot suggest the nature of punishment that should be meted out to the guilty persons. But it is sufficient to say that the punishment should be so as to deter the person and other persons of the same bent of mind from committing any crime against women. It should instil in them a sense of fear—a fear of prosecution and punishment.

The rising trend of violence against women has its roots in social insensitivity. Though there are sufficient legal provisions, their effectiveness lies in their implementation. The law enforcement agencies need to be made prompt and active in the implementation of laws.

Those who are responsible for implementing them have been found violating them. The need of the hour is that every segment of society should be sensitive and active against the violence against women.

The principle of 'eye for an eye', 'tooth for a tooth' had been the normal punishments in the good old days. In the present times, a similar schedule of punishment can be drawn up. Thus, if a person knows that he may lose a limb or his vital parts as the consequence of his evil deed against a woman, his conscience can be forced to act automatically to stop him from any such irrational action.

Another point that naturally comes out in such sombre and degrading situation is that our society should change its outlook towards a woman who has been through the traumatic experience of crime against her. She should receive the highest respect from the society. She should be at the centre of respect and reverence, instead of humiliation and antipathy. If we can mobilise enough public opinion, our society should call such women as martyrs.

Thank you.

❑ ❑ ❑

World Beauty Contest
(Speech by the Chairman of the Organising Committee)

Mr Chairman of the Jury of Judges, members of the Judges, Excellencies, honourable guests, ladies and gentlemen!

I have the honour to present to you a very glamorous pageant of beautiful ladies who have gathered here to participate in a competition being held here to select 'Beauty of the Year', i.e. Miss World.

These young girls, who are representing different cultures and countries will now pass before you in a parade of beauty. There are fifty-five most beautiful ladies from all over the world.

Ladies and gentlemen, mind you, these are not ordinary girls but the queens of their own countries—the

most beautiful girls, the pride of their nations. They have worn the crowns of beauty in their respective lands. I warmly welcome all of you girls and I wish you all the best!

Ladies and gentlemen, please give them a big hand as they pass before you on the stage.

I believe this type of contest promotes an awareness towards intelligence and beauty. These contests are very important in order to distinguish and find out the best beauties who are also endowed with best brains.

It is not only the beauty which is selected but also their intelligence has a decisive role in their selection. The questions they answer instantly without batting their eyelashes are much above the ordinary intelligence.

Also, the tests they go through would at once pronounce them as extraordinary human beings.

Our contest, ladies and gentlemen, is about to begin. I am sure, at the end of the contest we will have before us three young ladies—the winner, the first runner-up and the second runner-up who have in them the combination of the best beauties and the best brains.

Thank you.

❑ ❑ ❑

Fashion Parade
(Speech by the President of the Organising Committee)

Ladies and gentlemen!

Fashion parade in this modern age has acquired a great importance because today culture manifests itself in a blend of actions, gestures and postures. Fashion no longer remains confined to dress and style. In fact, it is a reflection of culture and civilization.

In recent times, fashion parade has become highly controversial. The controversy about 'Fashion Parade' is not yet over. People who have fundamentalist attitude oppose the organisation of such fashion show on the ground that such fashion parade will promote western culture in India. Hence not good for the values of our country. Getting over this controversy as to whether the Fashion Parade is good or not, I must add that a rich fare awaits you in which you will see the top models of the country displaying various garments which have been designed for this summer season by a well-known foreign designer. In fact, it is good for the promotion of business and commerce.

Since the hotel auditorium is comparatively small, we had no alternative but to restrict the number of audience for any show. However, the show will continue for four days and I think that this period will be enough to include all the interested visitors.

A dress that is hung on a showroom clay model, may look and sparkle differently when it is actually worn and displayed in walking, standing and so on. The fitting of the garment and the movements of the body within the garment are very much necessary to find out the desirability of the dress.

Ladies and gentlemen, I am sure that you will find our displayed garments interesting and of great taste. I also hope that our models will perform to the best of their skill and ability.

So, ladies and gentlemen, judge for yourself and enjoy the show.

Thank you.

❑ ❑ ❑

Motor Car Rally
(Speech by the Sponsor's Representative)

Ladies and gentlemen!

This vintage car rally has a long tradition in this city and it is being held here as the fifteenth such annual event. There are fifty participants in this rally and their car models date back to more than fifty years. The purpose of this car rally is a simple one to show man's love for antique things, i.e. cars.

As we know human beings have great fascination for cars for a long time. Some people are very passionate for the cars. They not only enjoy the riding of different models of car but also preserve them. As all ancient things have a beauty of their own, the passenger car is no exception. Besides providing us a glimpse of the development of automobile engineering and industry over the past decades, it also shows us the ingenuity with which the human mind first constructed this mode of transport.

In this rally, we have among us a 68 years old gentleman among the participants who has kept all along with him the first car which was gifted to him in his teens by his father.

Ladies and gentlemen, car models have changed and improved greatly and car speeds have broken records. However, our love for old cars still persists. Old is really gold.

Thank you and enjoy yourself.

❑ ❑ ❑

Vote of Thanks
(Speech by the Secretary of the Organising Committee)

Mr Chairman, honourable guests, respected participants Excellencies, ladies and gentlemen!

If remarks by the Press and attendance at the seminar are any indications, our seminar on human rights has been a great success. For this overwhelming success, I first of all, thank the sponsors and the participants at the seminar.

The participants who are eminent persons belonging to different walks of life, managed to attend this seminar cancelling their many preoccupations. Thus, they provided the seminar the benefits of their experience and erudition.

Our thanks are due to all members of national and

foreign delegation. However, we must, in the first place thank our honourable Ministers of government who, in spite of their important and tight schedules, were available for the inauguration and valedictory sessions.

Our thanks also go to the members of the Press and other media who have correctly reflected the views and decisions of the seminar. We are also thankful to our respected audience without whose presence the colour and glamour of the seminar would have been absent.

We also extend our thanks to all the ambassadors and the mission heads of all the foreign countries who attended the seminar. Also, the organising staff and every worker connected with the holding of the seminar are to have our gratitude and thanks.

Before I conclude, I thank you all once again for your cooperation. We will remember the contributions made by all towards the success of this seminar.

Thank you.

❑ ❑ ❑

Charity Performance
(Speech by the Secretary of the Organising Committee)

Mr Chairman, honourable patrons and guests, ladies and gentlemen!

I am happy to tell you that this performance that we are going to hold today, has been possible only through the active cooperation from all of you, from the public and also due to the untiring efforts of our volunteers and in fact, everyone connected with this performance.

The play that is going to be staged a few minutes from now, will be acted upon by famous actors and actresses without any consideration of material gains. It is only the noble cause which has motivated them to spare time from their busy schedules. If they had not given their names and if they had not taken part, it would not have been possible to raise funds. Therefore our thanks and

gratefulness go to them. We wish them more and more success in their lives.

Also, we are grateful to our patrons who motivated us to hold this performance when they learnt that the money was being raised for the training and education of disabled children so that they may become self-reliant when they grow up.

On learning about the motivation behind the charity, the general public has also contributed freely and enthusiastically. We have already had negotiations with the authorities to provide us bigger place including school, playground and hostel for these children.

If authorities provide us the major part of the funds, the remaining part of money can be raised from such charity shows in different cities of the country.

We, therefore, ladies and gentlemen, require your cooperation and goodwill to enable us to keep our spirits high. This will also enable us to provide resort and shelter to these less privileged children.

Thank you.

❑ ❑ ❑

On Joining as the College Principal

(Speech by the New Principal)

The outgoing principal, heads of departments, members of staff and ladies and gentlemen!

I have joined as the new principal of this college today. At the outset, I would like to pay my compliments to professor Mr Bryde, the outgoing principal. He has provided excellent guidance and leadership to the students and staff of this college.

My first priority as the principal of the college would be to ensure discipline in the college. The college authority will not tolerate any unruly behaviour or indiscipline in any activity of the college, though youthful outbursts and outlets of energy are acceptable within the decent limits.

As students your priority should be to seek academic excellence and physical development. This way you can fulfil your own dreams as well as the expectations of your well-wishers, teachers and parents.

Sound health is the greatest wealth and hence apart from the college gymnasium, I would like to open a health club attached to our college so that the students can get instructions and guidance on preservation and maintenance of good health.

I would also like to open cultural training centres where students with a flare for cultural activities can practise music and other arts. I will have the library rules tightened so that students go to the library not for idle chats but for reading and studying only.

College life is more free than that of the school. However, freedom has its limits and boundaries. I would like to ensure that limits to the freedom of students.

Acquiring knowledge is the first priority of the students for which you come to the college and you are required to keep this priority always in mind. With this purpose in view, I would like to introduce periodical examinations through which the academic performance of the students can be assessed.

Your well-being will be my first consideration as students are dear to all teachers. As your principal, it will be my obligation to help the needy students and those students who may face sudden or unforeseen financial crisis. I can assure you that the academic careers of such students will never be allowed to suffer. They will be provided with every possible help and assistance to grow in life.

I wish you all a very bright academic future with all-round development of your personality.

Thank you.

Addressing a Press Conference
(Speech by the Convener)

Mr Chairman and friends from the press!

You have been invited to meet the leader and other members of our delegation who will be visiting many countries to explore the possibilities of trade and business and to strengthen the ties between our country and other countries on bilateral terms.

Mr Robert, who is leading our delegation to various Asian and African countries, is a well known industrialist, having business interest in engineering goods, construction, textiles and hotels. We are sure that under his leadership, our delegation will do very well in foreign countries. The main objective of our delegation will be to explore the business potentialities and to strengthen bilateral ties. At the same time it would be necessary for

those foreign countries which our delegation will visit, to send their delegation to our country so that business interactions are promoted through a proper rapport.

Ladies and gentlemen, you will now be provided with slips. You can write down your question, your name and the newspaper, magazine or the news agency that you represent. You are then to raise your hands with the slip and your question shall be brought to our table and Mr Robert will answer your questions.

First question from the press—Do you have any preference for any country among those that you are visiting?

Mr. Robert—In fact, there is preference only for maximum returns within the legal framework in business. Hence, all countries regarding their economic prospects are equal to us.

Second question—Is there any special sector such as industry, agriculture or mining on which you will lay more stress?

Mr Robert—We would like to expand more in the industrial sector and the tourism sector, though we would treat all business prospects or ventures equally.

Third question—Is there any financial agreement such as double taxation exemption, banking facilities on your agenda?

Mr Robert—These financial agreements are important for smooth business operations.

During this visit, we will look into the existing bilateral system with each country and on our return we would suggest to our government about improvements wherever necessary.

Fourth question—Since you will be visiting many countries, would you seek advantage at the cost of loss or disadvantage to another country?

Mr Robert—We will never seek advantage in one country at the cost of loss or disadvantage to another country, whether situated far or near, that is our objective.

Fifth question—Why does your delegation not include representatives from important export industries such as leather, automobile, etc.?

Mr Robert—Ours is an exploratory mission and technically not an export promotion one. So, established export sectors have been kept out.

The convener—Ladies and gentlemen, though we would like to continue with such an important question–answer session, I am constrained to say that there are hosts of schedules and arrangements which are to be completed. So, friends we have to conclude this session now and we would welcome your best wishes for the success of our delegation abroad.

Thank you.

❑ ❑ ❑

On Taking Over as the President of the Traders' Association

Mr Chairman, respected members of traders association, and ladies and gentlemen!

At the outset, I wish to thank you all for the great honour that you have conferred on me today by electing me the President of North City Traders' Asssociation. Ladies and gentlemen, I am very grateful to you for the trust you have reposed in me.

I have confidence that your faith in me will guide me to get better performance of our Association. I am proud to announce that last year when I joined the Association, we made great progress. We opened many shops and also started other business activities in our area. I would request that more ladies with drive, skill and means

should join our Association to begin their business career in this part of the city.

Dear members, during the last few years, our Association has achieved much but there is much more to be achieved yet. First of all, we have to take up the issue with the concerned authorities to allow us to keep our shops and establishments open during all festival seasons—three or four hours after the statutory closing time. At present we are granted the extension only during the main religious festivals. However, there are many other festivals when our customers go back disappointed as they find our shutters closed.

Apart from this, we have to increase our membership contributions a little so that we can advertise about our shops and other products both in newspapers and television.

Also, we have to open one or two more toilets and drinking water stands in our shopping complex.

Friends, as you have put your trust in me, I have to request for one favour from you and—that is your consistent cooperation—without which we won't be able to make our complex as one of the best in our city. When we are able to do this, we shall be able to attract more customers and tourists to our shops.

Assuring you of my best services and attention to all your problems. You can look forward to a very happy future.

Thank you.

❑ ❑ ❑

On Taking Over as the Secretary of Labour Union

Mr Chairman and dear friends!

At the outset, I thank you all for selecting me as the secretary of this labour union. In fact, you have placed great responsibility on my shoulders. I assure you that I'll put my best efforts towards fulfilling my responsibilities to your best satisfaction.

Dear friends, you have chosen me to guide you and to fight for your rights. Labour and capital are the two main constituents of the production process and we are as much important to production as capital and business policies. In fact, it is the labour force which turns a plan into reality.

In every developed country, labour is much respected and enjoys a high standard of living, though it does not

want profits and fat bank balances or luxurious life style. What we want is the fulfilment of bare minimum necessities of life—food, clothing, shelter and some recreation to recharge our working capacity.

We must be able to recoup our physical strength due to exhaustion. Labour power or working energy is a worker's capital and this capital should be preserved.

Dear friends, it should be our endeavour to keep our capital, that is our labour, our working power, intact. That is our moral and legal right and we will certainly fight to uphold this right.

However, friends, we should not forget the reality that all rights have duties attached to them and rights and duties go together. Therefore, friends, we must perform our duties well so that we can claim our rights. Please remember this and the rest you can leave to me.

I'll leave no stone unturned to ensure that labour is not exploited and that they get the proper share of the total national revenues.

Praise be to our country and to our labour! Long live labour unity! Once again I thank you all.

On Joining as the Manager of the Company

Respected colleagues and staff of the company!

Today I have taken over as the manager of this company and today is the first day in my new office. On this auspicious day, I would like to meet all my staff members.

All of us have to work as part and parcel of a big machine. A big machine may have large components and it may have smaller or very minute parts like nuts and screws. The big machine will work smoothly only if all the parts are fitted well in their places.

Even if a cog or a screw is out of place, the machine will not work properly or may even stop functioning.

As all of us are parts of our company—some big and some small parts according to our status and workloads—

each one of us is important, as far as the efficient working of the machine is concerned.

If any one of us drops off or fails in our duties, this whole company, which is like a machine, will not function properly. My work here is not only to dictate and supervise but also to think and devise strategies by which the company may grow and make profits.

Unless there is more production, more sales and more profits, the company may lag behind others. Our goodwill will fall and our share prices will go down. Each activity is connected with the other and each step is followed by the other.

In order to ensure that the company does well, you will not neglect your duties in whatever the status or position you are working. This will leave me enough time to frame out policies for betterment of the company as a whole. Our remunerations, bonus, perquisites and all other considerations depend on the health of the company and on its perfect running. I hope you all are aware of these facts. We should always remember this. Let us all go back to our work, to our duties, and let us endeavour to help the company win laurels in national as well as international market.

That's all for now. I thank you very much.

❑ ❑ ❑

Soccer Championship
(Speech by the President of the Football Association)

Honourable Minister of Sports, respected guests, ladies and gentlemen!

It is a moment of joy and great privilege for me to announce the beginning of the prestigious National Soccer Championship in which sixteen teams from all over the country are going to participate.

National Soccer Championship was started ten years ago. The venue of the championship is changed every year from one city to another. All the teams which are going to participate in this championship have done well in their regional spheres. It is expected that they will bring out their best to excel in the competition when they clash and contest with one another at national level.

The main target of this championship is to ensure that the teams face competition on a larger scale to draw out their best to emerge as champion. Complementary tickets of this championship have been distributed to various schools, colleges and sports organisations so that our young who wish to make their career in sports and games may have opportunities to better their own performances from the instances of the senior soccer players of the country.

I hope that you will have a good flair of soccer entertainment during this championship.

Thank you and enjoy yourself.

❑ ❑ ❑

Women's Meeting

Honourable guests and ladies!

This meeting has been convened to discuss a few issues especially related to women.

Our intention is not to keep our menfolk out of our discussions and thoughts. However, we have to make it purely a ladies' affair for, we have a few ladies with us who will be telling you their tales of woes, sorrows, misery and helplessness.

There are so many distressed women here. These women who are mostly from rural or semi-urban areas as well as from poverty-stricken areas of the cities, may not be able to narrate their stories before men. Most of the women are semi-literate. These ladies have been found out and assisted by our volunteers and they have been

brought to us by-and-by. One of them has been deserted by her husband who has taken all her ornaments.

The other was criminally assaulted by her employer and the third was beaten black and blue by her in-laws. Besides these, there are some other women also who have expressed their wishes to our volunteers to come under our wings. However, as our resources are limited and their lives are not totally unbearable at the moment, we have advised them to continue for some more time. At the opportune time, we shall take them also under our care.

It is our main duty to rehabilitate these women and help them to find proper work so that the black clouds which have settled in their lives, disappear.

Hence, we have convened this meeting so that you can get acquainted with these unfortunate women, learn about their problems first hand and then help them in whatever way you can to better their lives.

I, therefore, request you all to explore your sources of influence and acquaintances to find them proper rehabilitation.

I thank you very much for attending this meeting.

Children's Society
(Speech by the Secretary)

Mr Chairman, ladies and gentlemen!

I am happy to apprise you of the fact that our Society, which has been catering to the development of children, has been working successfully and thriving because of the cooperation extended by you, the public and the parents.

Our primary aim is to bring up a child in various dimensions, as childhood is the most impressionable age. It has the ingredients of a soft clay which can be moulded in any way. It is the duty of the parents and society as a whole to create favourable atmosphere which can bring out the special talents, the particular inclinations and tendencies of a child so that they can be magnified to their fullest extent.

Our Society endeavours to find out special qualities hidden or lying in a child and bring them on the surface. We arrange for different diversions, different tests, opportunities and outlets for the child to awaken his sleeping faculty. We strive to provide a child various set-ups wherein a child, by involving himself in hobbies and interests of his choice can give full reins to his aspirations and wishes.

The children are provided various kinds of toys and books as well as materials for painting, drawing and for doing sculpture work. The children give vent to their interests through these work-plays. In this way the child himself and we too come to understand the line of work and affinity which the child likes most. Then we make suggestions to parents and schools regarding these tendencies.

However, ladies and gentlemen, you may realise that a target as envisaged by us can be much expanded if we have more money, material and space. We will, therefore, appeal to the parents and concerned authorities to extend their help and cooperation so that our mission can cover more and more children.

In order to encourage large scale participation, we have kept the children's membership fees very low. Now we will approach the authorities to grant us larger space and accommodation. Also, we would request the parents to help us by contributing for our project.

With such cooperation from parents and authorities, we are sure that our mission will proceed smoothly. When a child grows, his mental standard and performance level can be utilised towards nation's progress. A properly trained and skilled human being is the real resource of a nation.

Thank you.

❑ ❑ ❑

SECTION VI

Debates on Topical Issues

A debate is a contest, or, perhaps, like a game, where two or more speakers present their arguments and attempt to persuade one another. It is a discussion in which reasons are advanced either in favour or against some proposition. The formal presentation of a stated proposition and the opposition to it is usually followed by a vote.

Debate is a formal method of interactive and representational argument. It is a formal discussion of an issue at a public meeting. It is, in fact, a broader form of argument than logical argument. In a debate two or more speakers express opposing views and one side often prevails over the other by presenting a superior context and/or framework of the issue, which is more subtle and strategic.

In a formal debating contest, there are rules for people to discuss and decide on differences within a framework defining how they will interact. In a debate each speaker is allotted a fixed time to speak either in favour or against the topic. The result of a debate may be decided by audience vote, by judges or by some combination of the two.

The major goal of the study of debate is to develop ability to play from either position with equal ease. An experienced debator is quite comfortable with either proposition. However, it is an art which is to be developed with practice.

A good debate is characterised by clarity of thoughts, scientific applications of method, organised response to topic, polite way of presentation, etc. Clarity is undoubtedly very important for a good debate. Lack of clarity in debate may lead to varied interpretation by different people. Hence in a debate, use of terms should be avoided.

Besides, in a debate emotionally charged words should not be used. Certainly words like radicals, ethnic, etc. find no place in a rational debate. Similarly, personal attacks on your opponents are signs of intellectual bankruptcy. A debate based on logic and reason packed with facts, figures and data is sure to win the hearts of the audience.

Democracy is the Best Type of Government

A. Debator in Favour of the Motion

Mr Chairman, sir

It has been universally proved that democracy is the best type of government. In a democratic set-up, there is the rule of law. Democracy has been defined as the government of the people, by the people and for the people.

In most of the countries of the world, democratic types of governments have been functioning successfully. In such a set-up, the will of the people prevails. People elect their representatives for the state legislative assemblies and also for the parliament. They form their council of ministers which governs the country. The government is thus responsible for all its actions to the people.

General elections are usually held every five years and those who fail to perform according to the promises made at the time of elections and according to the expectations of the people, are thrown out of power.

In a democracy, the will of the majority is supreme. If six out of ten persons, are in favour of a decision, a resolution or an act, it is made a law and the state is governed according to the wishes of the majority.

In other types of governments such as monarchy, dictatorship or the governments by a few influential people, many flaws are found. In a dictatorship, it is the rule of one man who can dictate his terms and conditions according to his whims and fancies. As a result, the masses suffer because they have no one to approach in case any injustice is done to them.

In all types of governments, except democracy, the judiciary is just in the hands of a few persons and masses cannot expect justice from a dictator or from the rule of a few.

In many countries of the world where dictatorships or monarchies existed earlier, they have been replaced by the democracies. In Nepal, the rule of the king was replaced by democracy, though not without much violence perpetrated by the military and the police controlled by the monarch. In Maldives too, the democratic type of government has come to stay after decades of dictatorship.

In the present times, masses do not tolerate the governments run by one person or a few influential persons of the society. People want the basic fundamental rights of freedom of speech, and freedom to profess religion of their choice, with no discrimination based on sex, caste, community or creed. All these fundamental rights needed for the complete development of human personality can be possible only if there is democracy.

Sir, I conclude by saying that there is no other type of government which can provide maximum security and freedom to grow and prosper to its citizens except a democratic government.

B. Debator Against the Motion

Mr Chairman, sir

I don't agree that democracy is the best type of government. It is a universally established phenomenon that no two individuals have same views on anything. In a democracy, it is the view of the majority which win the battle. The very inception of a democratic set-up is full of flaws.

In democracy, if a person does not get majority votes, he loses the election. On the other hand, if the person of another party gets a few more votes, he is elected to the legislature—national or state, though the former may deserve to be a good administrator by virtues of his head and heart.

Similarly, a well-deserving party may lose the battle in the elections in a democracy and a party of not very qualified, intelligent and honest members may be voted to power particularly when masses are not well educated and aware of the programmes and policies of a particular party as we see in India. They are swayed by emotion exploited in the name of caste, creed, community and religion. More often than not the democratic system is full of corruption.

Generally contestants are financially very strong. They along with the financial support from their parties spend a lot of money in campaigns. They give cash and kind to the voters to cast votes in their favour. It would not be wrong to say that they buy their votes. Sometimes the voters are intimidated to cast their votes in favour of a particular candidate. Such contestants may not always be qualified, honest and deserving. However, with money power and muscle power they are able to manage their vote banks. They are ready to resort to any ignoble or clandestine means to grab power.

Besides, it is said that if six not-so-wise people support a viewpoint and four wise persons oppose a viewpoint, the viewpoint supported by more number of people will be accepted in a democracy because it is the will of the majority that wins. This is the biggest flaw of democracy.

In many democratic countries of the world particularly in developing countries, majority of the voters are semi-literate or illiterate, ignorant of the democratic process and know little about the persons who they are going to vote. Also, most of the electorates are in a dilemma about to whom they should cast their votes. In fact, they are not aware of the value of their votes. Such electorates seek the advice of their acquaintances and cast their votes according to the wishes of such acquaintances, not on their own which is guided more by emotion than by intellect.

Before the actual elections take place, a lot of noise pollution is created in campaigns and electioneering. Lots of money is spent on posters and banners and private and public property is defaced by sticking the posters. Traffic snarls are caused by the rallies which are taken out before the dates of polls.

On the other hand, the other types of governments do not have such flaws. No money is wasted in campaigns, no money-power and muscle-power play their roles. In a dictatorship, it is virtually a one-man power. Such a person knows what is good for the citizens and for the country. He need not seek the advice of a majority. He can himself take decisions and get them implemented.

In a monarchy, the monarch wields the power solely. He has a few advisors to advise him. Such types of governments always existed all over the world and they were quite successful. The king was able to look after the needs of the people of the kingdom better than most of the democratic governments are able to do today.

If the head of a country is educated, wise, intelligent and righteous, he himself is sufficient to provide the best governance. The more the people in a government, the more different viewpoints are there and the governance not so efficient and prompt. The whole system of governance in a democratic set-up is rather slow and time-taking. Things do not move as fast as they are often required to. Decisions cannot be taken expeditiously and people suffer. Bureaucracy which is part of a democracy is either very slow in action or indifferent to the problems of the people. In a democracy, quality is sacrificed at the cost of quantity because it is the government of majority. This type of government is full of flaws, afflicted with very high corruption, nepotism and favouritism and can hardly do any kind of good to its citizens who deserve it.

Sir, I therefore, conclude by saying that democracy is not the best type of government.

❑ ❑ ❑

Science cannot Tame Nature

A. Debator in Favour of the Motion

Mr Chairman, sir

It is right that science cannot tame nature. Although all inventions of science such as radio, transistors, electricity, telephones, computers, mobile phones, means of transport, namely buses, trains, aeroplanes, spacecrafts, big and small machinery are gifts of science to mankind. Science has done tremendous good in different fields of human existence.

Modern man is fully dependent on science. From the moment he leaves his bed to the time when he retires to sleep, he makes use of the scientific things. He cannot think of life without science.

Electric stove, bathing rod, cooking gas, scooter or car and the air conditioner in offices—all are the gifts of scientific development.

Ancient man was deprived of these facilities because science had not developed then. He lived in jungles and hunted animals for food and used barks and leaves of trees to cover his bodies.

Gradually man started living in communities; agriculture came into being and scientific development started. From the beginning of scientific development till today, science has made great progress in all fields of human existence.

However, in spite of overwhelming progress, science has completely failed to tame nature. Floods, earthquakes, hurricanes, landslides, cyclones and other natural calamities happened earlier and they continue to happen even today with same severity and intensity. Science has not been able to control such unforeseen calamities. It is still not able to make accurate predictions about their time and intensity. Tsunami and Rita killed lakhs of people, a few years ago.

It has been proved that the more the man interferes with nature, the more the destruction nature causes. The fury of nature is so great that science and scientists seem to be toys in its hand. It is better for scientists not to interfere with nature and make use of the scientific progress for the welfare of mankind. Tampering too much with nature and trying to find out the mysteries of nature have always led to more sorrows than joys.

The sun, the moon, the stars, the earth, water, the planets and flora and fauna are all the gifts of nature to man. Man cannot survive without these gifts.

However, exploring the sun, the moon, the stars and the planets may not be a positive step for the survival of man. Many deaths were caused when scientists tried to experiment with the hidden mysteries of nature.

Sir, I conclude by saying that taming nature is out of question and out of reach of any human being. So, it is better we leave nature on its own and do not interfere with it.

B. Debator Against the Motion

Mr Chairman, sir

My friend who spoke before me gave the impression that science has played no significant role in human life and that science cannot control nature. However, the reality is that it is only science that controls all human activity. Man is dependent on science so much so that without the word 'science', human existence is out of question. Nature is, and has been to a great extent, though not fully, tamed by science. Dams have been made on the rivers to contain the flow of water; devices have been developed to forecast cyclones, hurricanes, floods and earthquakes. Man has succeeded greatly in gaining control over the forces of nature. Man landed on the moon quite a few years ago, planets are being explored to find possibility of sustaining life there, spacecrafts have been sent into the space.

Many unexplored areas of nature have been either explored or are being explored by scientists. Even birth and deaths are in the hands of medical science. Physicians can foretell by what time a baby is expected in the world and by what time a serious patient will have his last breath. Nature remains nature only till the time science is unable to know its mysteries. But once they are known, the science is the ultimate controller and master of nature.

From a small electric bell to a spacecraft, all are wonders of science. Without science man would feel himself orphaned and would find life not worth living. Science and its benefits cannot be challenged by nature. There is, however, no doubt that if the gifts of science are used for destructive purposes by man, he will certainly be ruined.

Nuclear energy, the gift of science, should be used for the benefits of mankind. But if the same energy is used in making nuclear and hydrogen bombs, as was the case in Hiroshima and Nagasaki during World War II, when lakhs of people were killed, maimed and became handicapped, the blame certainly does not rest with the science. But, it is the mankind who decides how the wonders of science are to be used.

Today, everything is controlled by science. Through mobile phones one can communicate with any person sitting in any continent of the world. A few years ago, this facility was not available to man. Science has progressed by leaps and bounds and is still carrying out research in the areas which are yet unexplored.

Sir, therefore, I would conclude by saying that science has greatly tamed the forces of nature and objects of nature are to a great extent under the command and control of science.

Coedication is the Need of the Day

A. Debator in Favour of the Motion

Chairman, sir

Coeducation is the need of the day and no one can deny this reality. When students of both sexes study together in schools and colleges, they get an opportunity for the proper development of their personalities. They study and grow together. Interactions between the students of both sexes are essential for the growth of their personalities.

If there are segregated educational institutions, students remain shy and do not have the courage to talk to the persons of opposite sex, when they grow in years. A sort of negative complex develops in both the sexes which leads to many problems. The coeducational institutions help the students in getting over the inhibitions to mix and interact with the students of opposite sex. This interaction starts at the inception of one's educational career and continues till one completes secondary or higher education.

It has been generally found that those students who study in segregated—'boys' or 'girls'—institutions do not find a chance to share, mix or interact with the students of opposite sex. When they complete their education, they develop a feeling of 'prejudice' or 'distance' with the persons of opposite sex and this continues throughout their lives. Students studying in coeducational institutions do not have any such complex as they find the opposite sex as normal human beings. As they mix and share with the opposite sex, they have a balanced outlook on life.

Students coming out of segregated schools or institutions remain shy to talk to the persons of opposite sex. Sometimes they are not in a position to express themselves freely, if the person happens to be of the opposite sex in offices or while appearing for an interview for a job. This proves a great constraint in the growth of their career.

Sir, I want to conclude that it is only coeducation which is the need of the day so that we do not grow as students with one-sided personality and having so many complexes.

B. Debator Against the Motion

Mr chairman, sir

I do not agree that coeducation is the need of the day and it leads to the overall development of individual's personality. Coeducation should not exist at all because instead of devoting their time to studies, students studying in coeducational schools, colleges and other institutions get attracted towards each other from the very inception of their educational career and get distracted. In fact, this attraction of opposite sex so much affects them that sometimes their careers are spoilt.

They devote less time to studies at school and while on their way back home they discuss amongst themselves about the boys and girls studying with them or in other classes. Most of their time is lost in such useless talks. They become insincere to their studies.

There are many instances of school children studying even in middle standards falling in love with the opposite sex and thus neglecting their studies. In fact, at school level they are not mature enough to take things normally and thus spoil their careers. They vitiate the atmosphere at schools and create numerous problems for their parents who send them to study and do not have an iota of doubt that instead of acquiring knowledge at school, they are indulging in amorous behaviour. Students studying in secondary schools, colleges and higher educational institutions also fall victims to this evil of the attraction of the opposite sex and ruin their careers.

Sometimes a girl is emotionally involved with two or three boys and a boy is attracted to more than one girl. This leads to serious consequences often leading to skirmishes and fights between two groups. There are jealousies, ill-feelings and the desire to take revenge. Often this results in police cases and legal entanglements as a consequence to love triangles. School authorities and especially parents are put to a lot of incovenience because of their children. Sometimes the situation takes such a worst turn that heinous crimes like murders are committed out of revenge or jealousy. Coeducation which is spreading fast in rural as well as urban areas is responsible for many social vices.

Sir, on the other hand, the solution to all such problems is segregated educational schools, colleges and other higher educational institutions. In such institutions there are students of only one sex. They mix with each other, interact and derive maximum benefits in studies. Their minds are not distracted because there is no attraction of the opposite sex. They have to devote their time to studies whole-heartedly while at school and while on their way back home they have not to discuss about the opposite sex but either studies or general things.

Their minds remain calm and focused to their studies.

They are very sincere to their studies. Such students bring a good name to their schools and institutions with which they are associated and also to their parents. Such students complete their studies successfully and rise to great heights in their careers thereby doing good to the society as a whole.

Sir, there is another vice in coeducational institutions. It has been seen that in some schools, some male teachers sexually assault their female students. We frequently come across this type of news in media. Such instances are reported even in higher level educational institutions as well. Though such teachers are put behind the bars. My point here is not that all the male teachers resort to this practice. However, even one instance is sufficient to tarnish the image of coeducational schools, colleges or other institutions. Also, sometimes teachers are attracted to their students of opposite sex. Sometimes students get attracted to their teachers. This is a serious problem and can be done away with only if there are segregated educational institutions with teachers of the same sex.

Sir, I conclude by saying that there should exist only segregated educational institutions so that students can complete their education successfully and also many blots can be eliminated which exist in coeducational institutions.

Urban Life is Full of Joy

A. Debator in Favour of the Motion

Chairman, sir

I fully agree that urban life is full of joy. There are all kinds of facilities available in the cities. Most of the people lead luxurious lives. They have all amenities and comforts of the science and technology which are largely denied to people living in rural areas.

All types of entertainment facilities are there in big cities. There are parks, swimming pools, gyms, cinema halls, multiplexes, etc. All types of medical facilities are also available in big cities. There are hospitals—government as well as private—well equipped with the most modern equipment and facilities. Besides, there are numerous private nursing homes where the affluents can get quick and quality treatment.

From the academic point of view also, the urban living is very useful. There are many universities, colleges, private as well as government schools and professional institutions to cater to all types of aspirants. There are big libraries stacked with all types of books, magazines, journals and newspapers.

Urban life provides great opportunities to all the inhabitants to grow and prosper which we do not have in rural areas. There are numerous job opportunities in the cities best suited to the people of different skills and capabilities. More than government sector, the private entrepreneurs provide jobs to all types of job seekers whether they are looking for the jobs of peons or for managerial posts. Cities have everything for everybody.

The services of highly qualified engineers, doctors, architects, lawyers, educationists are available in cities. Also, there are highly qualified personnel in the corporate field. There are various training institutions where people from different fields of technology can upgrade their skills to meet the changing needs of their respective fields.

Various types of transportation facilities are available in cities. There are private as well as public vehicles which cater to the needs of various commuters. Commuting is not a problem in a city. In case of any emergency one has not to wait for long. Taxis, autorickshaws and other private vehicles are at the beck and call of the commuters.

Supply of all items of day-to-day needs such as grocery, cloth, vegetables, fruits and milk is readily available. One has not to travel a long distance to purchase different items. All things of daily requirements are available in the markets, malls and individual departmental stores.

Hence, I conclude by saying that the urban living is full of joy and contentment and is complete with all the amenities and facilities required by people from different walks of life.

B. Debator Against the Motion

Mr Chairman, sir

My friend who just spoke about the glories of living in cities is totally ignorant about the bliss which rural living provides.

In cities everything is artificial. Cities are full of air pollution, noise pollution and water pollution. The growing number of vehicles makes the dwellers of cities mad with noise. These vehicles emit lots of smoke which leads to different types of diseases—asthma, bronchitis and many other diseases of lungs. Besides, there is a lot of noise pollution created by this moving sea of vehicles. Noise pollution causes loss of concentration, irritability, mental disorder and loss of hearing. Honking also adds to the noise pollution.

In addition, a lots of noise is created by factories, wedding ceremonies and religious functions which are held more or less every day. There are traffic jams and traffic snarls in the cities. Sometimes it takes hours to commute a mere distance of a few kilometers. There is noise and only noise everywhere in the cities. Life becomes a virtual hell for city dwellers, especially those who are old, sick, infirm and weak.

Industrial waste causes a lot of water pollution. If there are any rivers in the cities, they are fully polluted because the wastes generated in factories and houses are flown into these rivers. People throw a lot of rubbish into such water bodies thus, contaminate the water, which becomes unfit for cooking and drinking.

There is a great rush everywhere in the city. Schools are flooded with applications of admission seekers. They are many times higher than the seats available there. Large queues are seen at ration shops and other places where items of daily requirements are sold at a little cheaper rate or at subsidised rate.

Most people living in big cities are self-centred and have no time for anybody. Their only aim is to earn and earn more wealth. They seek pleasure in material possessions and their only god is money and what money can buy. If a person arrives in a city from a far off village, he is put into a lot of inconvenience. No one is ready to help him—to guide him or to show him the way to a place which he wants to visit. In fact, this living is no living at all. A city life is completely devoid of social life. In fact, a city dweller does not live; he simply exists. He has no time for others.

There are occasional power cuts, water is in short supply particularly during the summer. Crimes such as rapes, murders, loots, dacoities, eve teasing and pick-pocketing are the order of the day. This certainly cannot be called a good living. There are hardly any healthy interactions among the inhabitants of cities.

Sir, on the other hand, the life of rural areas is worth living. There is no problem of pollution in the villages. There is no water pollution, no air pollution and no noise pollution. There are very few vehicles, hardly any factories and no source of noise pollution in the rural areas. There are no crowded places and microphones do not blare out noise in marriage ceremonies or religious congregations

The inhabitants of villages are innocent, unselfish, caring and know no treachery, deception, and falsehood. There are hardly any violent outbursts in villages. People in villages are always ready to help others in whatever way they can. They are full of fellow-feeling and are sympathetic and compassionate. There is comparatively less density of population in villages. Hence, complete peace and solace prevails in the rural areas.

It is not that all villages lack in medical and educational facilities. There are government and private schools and colleges in the villages. There are dispensaries and hospitals and villages have every facility needed for the existence of human beings.

The bigger the city the more lonely a person is. However, in rural areas people are well acquainted with each other and they embrace any newcomers whether they happen to come from a far-flung village or an urban area. They extend helping hands to all.

The air is fresh and clean here. Complete serenity prevails and people are hale and hearty unlike those in cities where most of the population is afflicted with one or the other disease caused by different types of pollution. No one is in a hurry and everyone leads a simple and relaxed life without having any type of hurry or stress. People share and care one another.

No eatables are adulterated. Everything is fresh and pure in the villages. There is potable water from the natural sources or supplied by the government authorities. Fresh vegetables, fruits, honey, eggs, meat and other items of daily need are available in plenty.

Sir, I conclude by saying that only rural life is worth living.

❑ ❑ ❑

Non-vegetarian Food is the Best for Health

A. Debator in Favour of the Motion

Chairman, sir

There is no doubt that if a person wants to remain healthy throughout his life, he should eat non-vegetarian food. Non-vegetarian food supplies us with the proteins, vitamins, carbohydrates and all other ingredients needed for a healthy living.

Meat-eaters are always found healthy. They are healthy not only physically but they have a healthy mind also. A healthy body has a healthy mind. Those who don't eat animal flesh are generally found weak—physically as well as mentally.

Persons in the armed forces are given a regular supply of non-vegetarian diet. This diet only keeps them physically fit. Soldiers' physical strength is tested not only when they are at war with an enemy country, but also they manifest this strength during peace times. When there are natural calamities such as earthquakes, floods or landslides, army men are called to help and rescue people. They do this work successfully and without getting fatigued. All this is attributed to a great extent to their non-vegetarian diet.

Ever since man came on this earth, animal flesh has been relished. In the ancient period man used to hunt wild animals for his food. Then agriculture had not advanced and man fully depended on wild animals for his food. Even with the advancement of agriculture and existence of all types of vegetarian foods, people eat animal flesh.

Animal flesh is very nutritious and cures many deficiency diseases particularly related to protein deficiency. From time immemorial the practice of consuming meat has been in vogue. It is not without any reason that majority of the people on this earth are non-vegetarians.

Vegetarian food lacks in vitamins, proteins and many other nutrients needed for full growth and development of personality. In most of the countries of the world non-vegetarian food is consumed by majority of people.

Physicians advise patients to resort to non-vegetarian diet if their ailments do not get cured. This food is good for overall health and fitness and one can consume such a diet throughout one's life. Sir, thus, I fully agree with the motion of the house that non-vegetarian food is the best for health.

B. Debator Against the Motion

Chairman, sir

My worthy friend who spoke before me about the unprecedented uses of non-vegetarian diet is not aware at all of the eating habits.

In fact, human body is not meant for consuming any type of flesh. Flesh is very harmful for body, mind and soul. Flesh increases only flesh and does numerous other harms to the body. All holy books speak volumes against the non-vegetarian food. Such food kills the soul of a person who eats it.

Instead of curing minor and major ailments, flesh eating causes many diseases which are ultimately cured by resorting to vegetarian diet.

Obesity, high blood pressure, blood sugar, diabetes and many other diseases such as heart problems, cancer and even heart attacks are caused by eating non-vegetarian food. It is only the vegetarian diet with less and less condiments which is needed for a healthy and happy living.

People who eat flesh are generally quick-tempered and resort to violence at the slightest pretext. On the other hand, vegetarian food cools the tempers and keeps the body, mind and heart balanced. Those who start eating meat, find many excuses to continue this diet. They develop the taste once and then there is no coming back. They develop no taste for vegetarian food and declare it to be a tasteless diet because non-vegetarian food is full of oils, condiments and chillies which are all harmful for heart, liver and other parts of the body.

There is a growing awareness among the people of the benefits of vegetarian food. People are switching from non-vegetarian food to vegetarian food in many countries where more and more flesh is eaten. After having eaten flesh for a very long time, they develop many physical and mental disorders and once they start eating vegetarian diet, they find that most of their disorders are automatically cured.

The notion that non-vegetarian food makes one healthy is totally baseless. On the other hand vegetarian food gives more vigour and vitality. Also, in non-vegetarian diet we kill those innocent animals who have done no harm to anyone. When they are butchered, they are not happy but with full of revenge and anger. Hence the flesh-eaters along with flesh also consume the curses of the dead animals and birds.

Hence, sir I fully support the vegetarian diet. It is the only diet which is worth consuming and not the non-vegetarian diet.

❑ ❑ ❑

Is there God?

A. Debator in Favour of the Motion

Mr Chairman, sir

There is no doubt that there is God. Everything is controlled by God. Nothing is in the hands of man. Even a leaf cannot move without His command. Death and birth are in the hands of God. The whole universe—the sun, the stars, the earth, all living, movable and immoveable things are the creations of God.

We see the presence of God in all human beings, in all animals, birds, and animate and inanimate things. The innocent faces of children reveal His presence. His presence can be felt in a grain of sand and in a big mountain. Only we must have the eye to see that everything is being controlled by God. The movements of all human beings, all animals and birds are in His hands.

The rustling winds, moving oceans, flowing rivers and even small ponds are under the control of God. He is the creator, the preserver and the destroyer of the whole universe.

Man has made great scientific development. He has sent men on the moon. He has created aeroplanes, computers, vehicles and the Mars is being explored by man. However, man has failed to create a flower. He can imitate but he cannot create. It is only God Who creates and His presence can be felt in the ant as well as in the elephant. What man only needs is to see God's presence in everything and he would have firm faith in the existence of the Almighty.

When a child is born, there is an automatic flow of milk in the mother's breast. This milk is neither too cold nor too hot, because the newborn baby cannot drink either, so the milk is according to the requirement of the newborn baby. The same is the case with all the newborn babies whether of human beings or of other animals or birds.

The question whether there is God or not is debated only by those who are atheists. It is God's blessing which is needed to believe in Him and it is denied to so many people who think that everything is done by man and God cannot do anything and therefore He has no existence.

However, those who have plunged into their inner selves, have realised His existence in all the system of things. Man cannot be born until God wishes and he cannot die until He wants to take away his last breath.

Hence, I conclude with deny the assertion that there is no God.

B. Debator Against the Motion

Mr Chairman, sir

My respected friend who spoke before me, fully justified his words that God does exist. For some people God may be there and He might be showering His blessing on a few persons like my friend who spoke before me.

However, taking into consideration the sorrows, sufferings, ailments and untimely deaths of numerous people—not only of the aged but also the young and the children—I firmly and emphatically believe that there was no God, there is no God and there will be no God in the future years.

Who has seen God? Is there any human being who can claim that he has seen God or has had a talk with Him. Had there been such thing as God, this earth would have been a happy place to live. There are innumerable sick persons in the hospitals. Patients suffering from mild ailments to very serious ailments remain admitted in various government hospitals and private nursing homes for years. Why can't God provide them some relief? We see everyday people dying in road accidents, air accidents and sea accidents. God does not spare even infants and children who are snatched away from this world before they have fully seen and realised what and how this world is.

The devotees who throng various temples and places of worship to offer prayers to their deities are killed in stampedes and terrorist attacks. If God exists and exists everywhere, why can't He come to the rescue of such unfortunate persons?

Sir, there is no God. People believe in the existence of God because of fear—fear of the unknown.

People feel that no tragedy should befall their children, other relations and near and dear ones. So they start feeling the existence of God out of fear. Had there been God, this world would be a slightly better place to live in. The innocent are looted and murdered in cold blood, children are orphaned, wives become widows and husbands become widowers before time. Why is there so much suffering on this earth if there is God?

If people are cautious about their *Karmas* (deeds) and if they do only the righteous deeds, the sufferings of human beings will certainly lessen.

Sometimes people suffer because of the evil deeds done by them in their previous births. Many people suffer because they resort to crime, fraud, treachery, deception violence and untruth. If people do righteous deeds, their sufferings will automatically diminish. This is the law of nature.

Sir, though the existence of God is doubtful and controversial, one can enjoy the fruits of a happy living if one is in touch with nature. If there is God why is He a silent spectator? Why is He mute? Why does His heart not melt on seeing the heart-rending cries of the sufferers?

Man's birth, his growth, old age, weakness and death—all these are natural processes and God does not play any role in any of them.

Only weak persons believe in the existence of God. Those who are physically, mentally and emotionally strong, can lead happy lives. They do not search for God when a misfortune knocks at their door. They think, act and implement their decisions firmly and strongly and are thus able to come out of any misfortune or bad period of their lives.

Hence, I conclude emphatically that God does not exist.

❑ ❑ ❑

Divorce is a Curse or Boon

A. Debator Against the Motion

Mr Chairman, sir

Before I speak on divorce, we should all recall wedding ceremony—the night when two throbbing, pulsating hearts meet and they are tied in wedlock.

And before that, marriage vows are taken before the altar or the holy fire and these sacred ceremonies are organised and rituals are performed to bring the two young hearts together and bind them in matrimonial ties. Then they are pronounced as husband and wife.

The hopes and aspirations of this young couple, their glorious aim of raising an ideal family and to establish themselves as a vital and vibrant unit of society—all such dreams can be fulfilled if the legal barricade known as divorce does not exist.

I don't understand why the word 'divorce' exists at all, who coined it and who implemented the divorce laws.

In fact, divorce is the bane for married life. This vicious bogey is a great threat to a peaceful married life. It shakes the very foundation of a happy married life often separating the two souls permanently who have vowed for a lasting relationship. Sometimes all efforts of the well-wishers to patch up their differences, quarrels to save the marriage fall flat.

Sir, no worse evil can exist than divorce which destroys the life of a man, a woman, their children and rather the whole family. The family is shredded and scattered to the wind and the life of children who are the future of society, is crushed before it blooms. No doubt, there are social organisations and welfare societies which have reconciliatory roles but unfortunately none has been too effective to root out this evil—divorce—from society. It is, no doubt, the greatest vice of our personal and social life which is the greatest threat to the basic unit of society—family.

It is fate and the divine power which bind the marriage knot between a male and a female. Then there is the thrill of married life, the experience, the small and big adjustments that turn very sweet with the passage of time. The petty and periodical outbursts of temper appear as child's play.

I think we should do away with the system of divorce and all sensible persons will certainly support my view point.

Mr Chairman, sir, I have had my say but my voice chokes when I visualise the flame and the catastrophe that divorce brings to our society particularly in the life of a woman, who is looked down upon as an outcast. I will not rest in peace till I have not contributed to eliminate this monstrous law of divorce.

B. Debator in Favour of the Motion

Mr Chairman, sir

I appreciate the speaker for his high sounding words. However, these words were certainly hollow from inside. His speech, no doubt, was impressive but only from imaginative perspective and lacked practical overtones. The way my friend spoke depicted the treacle toffee life of a married couple. In fact, he had no glimpse, no insight, into the life of a married couple, sweet and sour to quote his words.

The pulsating and throbbing brides on the wedding night and the nupital bed of the Arabian tales are true indeed for many couples. However, he has no knowledge of many more throbbing brides whose pulsating married first nights have turned into tremor-struck horror, when they found their life partners, their revered husbands coming in a drunken state with wobbling feet and trembling hands—hands that trembled not with adulation or excitement but with worthlessness. If this is the beginning of a married life which is the stark reality for many brides, there can never be expected high hopes, lofty ideals and the bridal aspirations.

I am sorry to point out that my friend failed miserably to paint the picture of married life in its true colour. It is not the question of occasional bickerings, tiffs and tussels that may lead one partner or the other or both to become desperate enough to sever the ties of wedlock.

The considerations for divorce may go much deeper into the behavioural patterns of a husband or wife, their mental agonies, miseries and frustrations, their physical torture and oppressions, their literal enslavement and distortion of personality

Sir, if we exclude a few criminal-minded and designing women from the purview of the whole lot of the women race, the woman stands as the symbol of motherhood and procreator of mankind. She deserves to be loved and respected. Unfortunately, often marriage proves a cause of her miseries and endless woes. It is the divorce which provides her an escape from the marriage and saves her from torture.

However, every person has a right to live honourably, respectfully, to fulfil herself or himself, to bring out the best in her or him in order to shine and rise in the society.

When these prospects are mercilessly cut short by one partner, to subjugate the other—to possess the other's body, heart and soul, when ill-treatment is meted out to this partner, when living every moment turns into a curse, a living death, then there is no alternative for the state, the society, for the well-wishers to intervene to protect the hapless and darkened souls and extricate them from the tentacles and clutches of their persecutors.

Hence, I can emphatically say that divorce is a social saviour, a gift for the miserable and a boon for a ruptured marriage.

❑ ❑ ❑

Honesty is the Best Policy

A. Debator Against the Motion

Mr Chairman, sir

'Honesty is the best policy' is an old, outdated and obsolete saying. Such a policy is best left to preach and not to practise; or it may form part of the moral or ethical teachings in schools.

In the modern times those persons who are honest are the worst sufferers. They are cheated, fooled and hoodwinked. On the other hand, those who are dishonest, are able to lead better lives. Modern time is the time of dishonesty. Rather the adage should go "dishonesty is the best policy today".

We see in our day-to-day life that those who resort to honest ways of life do not earn better, do not live better and are not able to maintain even moderate standard of living. However, those who resort to dishonest ways earn more and more money and lead better lives. They are able to provide best education to their children. They move in high-profile society, visit best hotels, restaurants, clubs and other places of entertainment. Such persons enjoy all the luxuries of life.

If we keep on talking that honesty is the best policy and follow this principle, we may not be able to make our both ends meet, not to talk of enjoying luxuries of life.

Only those who don't get a chance to earn money through dishonest means say that honesty is the best policy. If such people get an opportunity to get money by dishonest means, they will stop saying that honesty is the best policy. There might be times in the olden days when people were honest. They might not be resorting to dishonesty because people then were scared of the unknown powers. They thought if they did anything dishonest, Almighty would be angry with them and thus punish them in so many different ways. This might be the only reason why people were afraid of doing anything bad, evil or dishonest.

However, as the science has fully developed in the modern times, people know that there is no unseen power which can punish us if we do something wrong.

I can quote so many examples where people have made great progress and have risen in status by dishonest means. They have accumulated lots of money through dishonest means. These people are living happy lives. No power has punished them. They are hale and hearty, their children are also leading healthy and prosperous lives.

Even to earn the bare minimum needs of life is difficult rather impossible, if one sticks to the norm of 'honesty is the best policy'. Everyone has to resort to dishonest means one day or the other, only one waits for the opportune time to get the right opportunity.

Sir, I, therefore, very strongly and emphatically declare that no one can follow the principle of 'honesty is the best policy' in the modern times.

B. Debator in Favour of the Motion

Mr Chairman, sir,

I do not agree with my friend who spoke very emphatically and declared that no one can stick to the principle of ‘honesty is the best policy’ in the modern times.

I, however, regret to point out that my dear friend has been associating with wrong persons whose only aim is to amass more and to gain more money and other material wealth which according to him lead to a better and prosperous life. Perhaps he must not have come across noble people.

There is no doubt that those who resort to dishonest ways to earn money or to rise in status, enjoy life for some time. They think that by resorting to dishonest means, they have achieved everything in life. However, such happiness is temporary and ephemeral. In no times of human history man has been able to get lasting happiness by resorting to dishonest means. This happiness is elusive and does not last long.

Such people have to reap the harvest of their sowing. “What we sow, so shall be reap.” This proverb was made hundreds years ago and it is true today also. Whatever the times of human history, we know that those who did not follow the norm of honesty in any field of their lives, suffered terribly.

Such sufferings came not at once but they did come surely with the passage of time. Those who earned more and more money by dishonest means suffered in so many different ways.

Even today persons resorting to dishonest ways in their lives suffer slowly but surely. This is manifested in varied forms either as affliction or misfortunes that befall on the family. Their spouses are afflicted with one or the other fatal diseases, their offsprings have to bear the brunt of their parents’ doings and they lead very unhappy lives.

Only those who, in spite of many opportunities, to earn through dishonest means or to rise in life in any field through dishonest ways, stick to honesty, enjoy lasting happiness. They may not be having palatial houses and fat bank balances, but their life is worth living. They experience inner peace and they enjoy complete solace which is denied to the persons who are dishonest.

This world is running smoothly only because of the existence of some honest persons on this earth, though their number may not be large. If all human beings are of dishonest tendencies and inclinations, this world will perish completely in no time.

All persons who are God-fearing, religious-minded, read scriptures and follow the dictates of the holy books and listen to the sermons of saints, never do anything in their lives, which smack of dishonesty.

The fruits of dishonesty may look wonderful but this wonder is shortlived and the sorrows and sufferings which follow them are so painful and agonising that dishonest persons, after doing their deeds repent and repent repeatedly and terribly but alas! The time gone never comes back. What has been done can never be undone. Their only fate is to suffer and suffer and burn in the fire of their misdeeds. They keep suffering till they glide to the grave.

Sir, I declare emphatically that all human beings on this earth should resort to only honest ways and should not be lured to any kind of dishonest means of earning money or gaining any type of material benefit because these are shortlived and will certainly lead to a ditch of darkness.

❑ ❑ ❑

Dowry System is a Vice

A. Debator in Favour of the Motion

Mr Chairman, sir

I fully support the motion that dowry system is a vice. There is no doubt that the custom of giving dowry to the bride by her parents is in vogue since time immemorial. However, this custom was a sacred custom a few years ago and the family of the bridegroom willingly accepted whatever dowry was given by the family of the bride. Then it was not considered as an evil and the newly-wed couple started their married life on a happy note. However, this custom has been exploited in the present times. Now giving dowry and accepting dowry has become a big social evil.

The rich in the society feel it their prestige to give a lot of dowry in cash and kind. Affluent parents give a lot of money as dowry to the bridegrooms. A lot of money is spent in decoration, lighting arrangement and other things. For them it is an opportunity to show off their wealth. This is a sheer wastage of money and nothing but a mere show-off.

Such an attitude promotes the practice of dowry in society. Sometimes big demands are made by the parents of the bridegrooms before the marriage. Their demands are easily met by those families which are rich. However, the parents of the poor girls cannot afford dowry and they have to suffer a lot.

Big loans are taken, sometimes, by the parents of the poor girls in order to fulfil the demands of the bridegrooms. It becomes difficult to repay these loans. Such parents are burdened greatly and have to undergo severe financial crisis after their daughters are married off.

Poor parents are the worst sufferers of dowry system. We hear more or less everyday that women are ill-treated, tortured and even burnt alive for not bringing sufficient dowry. The greed of some bridegrooms and their parents keeps on increasing everyday. The newly-married women are sent to their parents' home to bring more and more items of dowry or money. These demands never end. There is greed for more and more and many women who cannot fulfil these demands, are either forced to put an end to their lives or put to death by their spouse or in-laws.

This is a big blot in the society. Marriage is a sacred ceremony. It is the union of two bodies and souls. In fact, nothing should be demanded in dowry. Although there are acts and regulations against giving and taking of dowry, this evil practice continues. The rich people who give and accept dowry, do it clandestinely and do not make it public.

Sometimes, cash is demanded by the parents of the boys a few months before the marriage takes place. This demand is based on the educational qualification and social status of the boys. The demand is very high if the boys are engineers, doctors, big businessmen or if they are working as senior executives in government or private sectors. In fact, marriage has become a trade in the modern times. This sacred union has acquired a wrong meaning in materialist society of today, In fact, the boys are sold as commodity against money. The basic purpose of marriage has been distorted.

Sir, I conclude by saying that dowry system is a stigma in any society and this custom of giving and taking of dowry should be done away with. Those who demand dowry should be dealth with strictly so as to create a society free from this evil.

B. Debator Against the Motion

Mr Chairman, sir

I have different views from those of my friend who declared that dowry system is a vice. In fact, giving and accepting dowry is a very sacred tradition. Dowry has been given and accepted ever since the inception of the institution of marriage.

All parents on this earth want to give something—in cash or kind—according to their capacity, to their dear daughter who is going to be married and start a new life.

Dowry is meant to help the newly-married couples to start their life. No parents on this earth want that their daughter to go to her groom's house empty-handed. In fact, the custom of giving dowry has always existed and will always exist. This custom cannot be checked or stopped by any law or regulation.

However, the demand for dowry usually made by the bridegroom is wrong. Those who demand huge dowry should not be encouraged. These days, there have been numerous instances where the girls have refused to marry the boys who demanded dowry.

The demand for dowry reflects the greed hence, it should be discouraged. If there is no demand from the parents of the boy, the girl's parents have every right to give cash or kind, according to their capacity, to their departing daughter.

Dowry as such is not an evil and this system of giving and taking dowry is considered as a sacred system. In fact, the affluent parents have distorted this pious tradition of dowry. They want to show off to their relations and neighbours that they have a lot of wealth and that they can give so much dowry to their daughters that no other parents can have a parallel to their wealth. Such a practice should be discouraged for it promotes those who are greedy. They take marriage an opportunity to get more and more money and wealth. In such a competition, the poor parents are put to a lot of inconvenience and agony.

Sir, therefore, I would like to conclude by saying that giving dowry by a girl's parents is no crime at all. Dowry should not be encouraged where there is demand and greed accompanied to it.

❑ ❑ ❑

Beauty Contests Should Be Banned

A. Debator in Favour of the Motion

Chairman, sir

I fully support the motion that beauty contests should be banned all over the world. A lot of national money is wasted in holding these beauty contests. There are different beauty contests—Miss University Contest, Miss Universe Contest, Miss World Contest—and more or less every country of the world individually holds beauty contest.

Women parade before a large number of people of both the sexes in semi-naked dresses and show their bodies to be selected as Miss World or Miss Universe, First Runner-up and the Second Runner-up.

This whole practice is immoral and unethical. Holding of beauty contests clearly manifests the deterioration of moral values. In the olden days there were no such contests because no woman belonging to any part of the world wanted to show her body to the people. But in modern society of today women do not hesitate to uncover their bodies and make a show of them. This is the degradation of womanhood and also a decline in moral values of society.

Moreover, the money which is lavishly spent in holding these contests can be utilised in the welfare of the society. Many under-developed and poor countries also hold these beauty contests. There is a lot of poverty in these countries and many people are not able to make even both ends meet. Holding these beauty contests is a shame for such countries.

The host countries of these contests have to make different arrangements for holding these contests such as security arrangement, accommodation, etc. and money is spent extravagantly. The same money can be used to lessen the sufferings of the poor, downtrodden and the less-privileged. The money can be utilised in social sector or it can be used to set up industries or develop infrastructure. It will greatly lessen the woes of the people, and help in making the life of the people better.

Sir, I therefore, conclude by saying that these beauty contests reflect nothing but degradation of civilizational values and wastage of public money, hence should be banned completely.

B. Debator Against the Motion

Mr Chairman, sir

My views are different from those of my friend who strongly opposed the holding of beauty contests and also suggested that such contests should be banned immediately world over.

Sir, it seems that my friend who spoke before me still has the pattern of thinking of medieval period. We are progressing day by day, the whole civilization of the world is advancing and there is an air of modernity in all walks of human existence.

There is, in fact, no harm in holding these beauty contests. Such contests have numerous benefits. These contests provide a stage where women and people of different countries meet and interact with one another which provides an opportunity to learn about the cultures of different countries.

These contests also offer an opportunity to different aspirants of various countries who want to excel not only in physical beauty but also in the beauty of brains. Thus, these contests do not merely centre around the beauty of the skin but also provide a ground where the mental calibre of the contestants is assessed. Thus they promote a healthy competition.

Besides, the contestants are put to various other tests to know whether they possess the human and humane qualities of human heart and mind.

The money collected by holding these contests is spent in the welfare of society. This money is spent in opening hospitals, orphanages and homes for the aged. This is not at all the wastage of national money. On the contrary, money collected through these contests is put to the best use—the service of humanity.

Young women, through these contests, are encouraged to participate in national and international events to manifest the beauty of the bodies, minds, hearts and souls. Such contests should be a regular feature which should be promoted right from the school level to national and international level.

The contestants get many opportunities on national and international level to interact with one another and to know more and more about regional and international languages, traditions, cultures and civilizations.

Sir, I, therefore, emphatically declare that such beauty contests should be regularly held nationally and internationally.

❑ ❑ ❑

Spare the Rod and Spoil the Child

A. Debator in Favour of the Motion

Chairman, sir

I fully support the motion—'spare the rod and spoil the child'. Children must not always be treated very softly. There is no doubt that with the spread of education and awareness and development of culture, very less punishment is given to the children. They are not treated strictly either at home or at school.

In the ancient times, teachers and parents used to be very strict with children. Children were punished if they did not do well in studies or if they disobeyed teachers or parents. The children then grew up in the disciplined atmosphere. They were obedient, well-behaved and hardly ever dared to disobey teachers or parents. They were taught strict discipline at school and at home. Thus their grooming was perfect and there was an all-round development of their personalities, when they grew up.

However, with the passage of time and with the development of civilised society, attitudes of parents and teachers changed greatly. They became very lenient towards the children. The same is the case at present times. The results are here before all of us. By giving more love and less physical punishment to children, we have in fact, spoiled them. We find that the children of today are disobedient, arrogant, indisciplined and lack respect for teachers, parents and other elderly members of the society.

This is attributed to the fact that we are sparing the rod and spoiling the children.

Children should be very strictly dealt with if they do not show respect to parents, teachers or other members of the society.

Some regulations such as no physical punishment to the children at school, even if they do something terribly wrong, are also responsible for the flawed upbringing of children.

Earlier teachers were at liberty to punish students physically if they did not fare well in studies or if they violated any discipline.

However, with the enactment of lenient laws about punishing students, we are facing a lot of problem. In fact, initially it was thought wise not to punish children at school as we are a civilised society now. And that children would willingly follow discipline, obey laws and show respect to teachers, parents and other members of the society. However, this did not happen and children misused this liberty to become disobedient, indisciplined and wayward.

Sir, as the sparing of the rod has led to serious problems, I declare strongly that the rod should not be completely spared and in deserving cases, the children should be punished in order to put them on the right track of good life.

B. Debator Against the Motion

Chairman, sir

I have different opinions with those of my friend who spoke before me and emphatically declared that the rod should not be spared and the children should be given physical punishment so that we can improve them and groom them to become good human beings.

However, I strongly feel that we are not living in dark

ages and uncivilised society. Children of present times are quite sensible and sensitive. If they are punished physically, they will develop signs of negative thinking and it will hamper their natural growth.

Children are like young saplings. They should be made to grow a natural growth. If a sapling is made to grow naturally, it becomes a good plant and a great tree having strong branches and green leaves. If its growth is hampered by giving it out unnatural treatment, it will dry and wither. It cannot grow into a strong tree.

Similarly, children should not be interfered too much in their natural growth. Punishing children physically for every minor and major mistake, will not help them grow naturally. Children should be taught from the very beginning what is good and what is not good for them. This way they can understand the world and they will develop positive traits of personality.

Gone are the days when children were beaten blue and black for their minor mistakes or offences. We can not treat children like animals. Even animals are treated with love and compassion today. Children have to become independent and responsible citizens when they grow up and we cannot make them so if they are meted out physical punishment at every stage of their growth. Strict treatment is likely to lead them to negative thinking.

There are many instances to prove my point. Many children who are given physical punishment at home and school do not develop a positive personality. They develop an inferiority complex and this leads to their stunted growth. They find that everything is wrong and negative in this world. They become sceptic and synic and throughout their lives they suffer and remain victims of this negative development. It has a bearing on their behaviour. Their behaviour is not good with their family, friends and society as well.

We should, therefore, treat children softly, mildly and with a great caution. Children are very imitative by nature. They do the same as they see around them. They follow their elders and also people whom they meet and interact with. So we should have love, affections and care for them in our treatment. We should inculcate in them good habits with love and not by force. Giving children physical punishment will certainly harm them not only physically but mentally and psychologically also. It is most likely to affect the balanced growth of their personalities.

Sir, I fully declare that 'spare the rod and spoil the child' is an old, obsolete and outdated adage which holds no significance in aware and educated society of today. Hence, it should not be followed in the present times.

❑ ❑ ❑

Pre-natal Sex Determination is a Sin

A. Debator in Favour of the Motion

Mr Chairman, sir

I fully agree that sex determination is a sin. It is a sin not only against humanity but also against the will of the Almighty.

Many pregnant women undergo test to ascertain whether the embryo is a male or female one. If it is found to be a female embryo in the test, it is aborted. This is not only a great crime but also an unpardonable sin. A female embryo which was to become a female child as destined by God, is killed before it is made to see the world.

Life and death are in the hands of God and no human being has the right to prevent a birth. In the modern so-called civilised world, we are, unfortunately, resorting to many uncivilised and unethical deeds. Sex determination is one such deed.

If we have only male children and we get all the female embryos aborted, this will create a very big problem. Male and female ratio will be terribly disturbed and there will be hardly any females left in the world. This is revealed in the latest census report which shows a declining trend in male-female ratio. In fact it is a cause of great concern for government and society. Many state governments have launched campaigns against this evil practice. Goverments, with the help of some monetary benefits and other incentives, are trying to check the decline in sex ratio.

Many women belonging to the affluent families undergo pre-natal sex determination tests to find out the sex of the child and kill the child if found female before it comes into this world. Although there are laws according to which sex determination cannot be carried out and those who undergo this test may be punished, yet these laws are not strictly enforced and many surgeons abort the unwanted baby embryos clandestinely. As the greed for possessing more and more money is increasing in the modern world, these unscrupulous surgeons carry out these operations to earn quick and more money. Though with the spread of education the attitude of society has changed greatly. However, such evil practice of sex determination is now frequently reported in semi-urban and even in urban areas.

It is an irony that the practice of sex-determination test is more frequent in the so-called educated and aware section of society than the lower class. It has been found that many women belonging to the poor families hardly go for sex-determination tests and don't resort to sinful activity of getting the unwanted embryos aborted. They think that child is the gift of the Almighty and it should be allowed to see the light of the world whether it is a male child or female child. This thinking is ethical and accepted by the righteous persons. This needs to be propagated in every section of society.

Sir, I firmly believe that sex determination and abortion of any embryo whether it is male or female, are the biggest crimes and those involved in these sinful activities, must be strongly punished.

B. Debator Against the Motion

Chairman, sir

I differ with my friend who strongly condemned the sex-determination tests and abortions of the unwanted embryos.

However, I strongly feel that sex-determination test should be legalised in all the countries of the world. In fact, sex-determination test has a significant role to play in controlling the ever-rising population of the world particularly in some developing countries like India and China where parents have a desire to have a male child out of some religious and social practices prevalent in respective societies.

Women should have the right to go for this test. Many women after having a few female babies want to put a stop to having more and more female children. If such women undergo sex-determination test to know whether the unborn baby is a male or female and if the female embryo is aborted, I don't think this is a sinful act. On the other hand, it is a positive step towards controlling increasing birthrate. In most of the cases it has been observed in India that out of her own desire or family pressure to have a male child a woman continues to have babies. This is one of the major causes of population growth in India. Through sex determination, mothers can have wanted children whether they are male or female and unwanted children can be avoided.

Further, the question is not of affluent families and poor families. My worthy friend who spoke before me was of the view that most of the poor families do not gor for this test and thus allow all children to come to this world. Here I would like to point it out that this certainly is a negative step towards population control.

It has been seen that unaware families have more and more children. Though by not undergoing sex-determination tests, the families may not be resorting to unethical deed, yet they are the only ones who are responsible for population explosion of the world. The poor parents having more and more children, are not able to even properly feed them. They do not have sufficient resources to educate their children either. Such children are not sent to school. They are left to fend for themselves. As a result, many such children work as domestic helps or they are compelled to work in small restaurants, shops or in factories. This contributes to the problem of child labour. When they should be playing and going to school, they have to do manual work for which they are hardly paid a pittance. Their future becomes dark and remains sealed throughout their lives. These children who should be the human resources of the country turn out to be a liability to the nation, due to lack of proper education and training.

Therefore, it is better to have less children so that they can be fed, clothed, educated and made to lead a decent and honourable life.

Sir, I therefore strongly feel that all women should be given the legal right to carry out the pre-natal sex-determination tests so that they can have a control over the size of their families.

Cable T.V. is a Nuisance

A. Debator in Favour of the Motion

Mr Chairman, sir

I fully agree that Cable T.V. is a nuisance. In fact, it is a 24-hour nuisance.

Cable T.V. is responsible for spoiling many youths. Earlier national channels of different countries used to telecast various programmes on national T.V. network. Such programmes used to convey very interesting and patriotic messages. Besides, different tele-serials were also packed with some moral or ethical messages for the young, the old and other people from all walks of life. The timings of the telecasts were limited and controlled.

However, with the advent of Cable T.V. there are numerous channels which telecast various programmes every moment round the clock. Cable T.V. has seriously affected the studies of the students. They remain glued to T.V. sets for most of the time and care little for their studies. This adversely affects their educational career. Many parents who know the disadvantages of Cable T.V., have to virtually snatch the remotes from the children's hands and switch off the T.V. sets. This leads to many other problems. Sometimes children begin to feel antagonism towards their parents. Often they turn violent against their parents for not allowing them to watch T.V. continuously.

Young students who are just at the inception of their educational career are not mature enough to know what programmes are good for them and what are not. They fail to listen to the advice of their parents as to how much

T.V. they should watch, and how much time they should devote to their studies so as to make their careers.

Some programmes which are telecast on Cable T.V. are not worth watching. Children are more attracted to such programmes. Whenever their parents are away from home or whenever they get an opportunity, they watch these programmes. This corrupts their minds and affects their studies.

There are movies which are only for the adults. These are not good for the immature children. Children, however, watch many 'only for adults' movies and other programmes which has negative impacts on their minds. Cable T.V. has not only adversely affected the career of students but also the adults. Many adults also become addicted to watching different programmes of their choice on T.V. and neglect their work. Many housewives too watch Cable T.V. invariably and regularly and neglect their household work. Also, Cable T.V. has seriously affected the social lives of individuals. It has been seen that the continuous and 24-hour telecasting of programmes make the viewers continue watching T.V. even if a guest drops in. In fact, the coming of guest becomes a cause of displeasure for them. They feel disturbed and the guest has the impression that he is an unwanted person.

Sir, I therefore, conclude by saying that Cable T.V. is a real nuisance adversely affecting the lives not only of children but also of students, women and even elderly persons.

B. Debator Against the Motion

Mr Chairman, sir

My worthy friend who spoke before me firmly declared that Cable T.V. is a nuisance, rather a 24-hour nuisance.

In fact, Cable T.V. has revolutionised the lives of all individuals. Before the advent of Cable T.V., only boring and lacklustre programmes were telecast by the national T.V. channels of various countries. There was no choice and the viewers were compelled to watch whatever was being telecast. This is not the case with the coming of Cable T.V. There are numerous programmes which are telecast and the viewers of all ages have the choice to watch the programmes according to their taste and liking.

In fact, Cable T.V. is not a 24-hour nuisance but it is a good source of 24-hour entertainment and information. It is wrong to say that the programmes spoil the children. But, it is we the viewers who are responsible for what we do. The programmes of Cable T.V. are full of information, entertainment and learning. On viewing the programmes, you get an opportunity to learn about the culture, tradition, and cutoms of people of different countries. So far as the watching of Cable T.V. by children and students is concerned, it is up to the parents to guide their children to watch particular programme and not watch certain programmes. Parents can single out the programmes for the children and can strictly instruct them to watch these particular programmes only.

Life has, indeed, undergone a sea change. People now work in 24-hour shifts. Some employees have no time to watch T.V. during the day time when they are busy in their offices. They can entertain themselves during the late evenings or night hours when they are free.

Similarly, employees who work in night shifts can watch the programmes of their choice during the day time on Cable T.V. Earlier this facility was not available when Cable T.V. was not there. Now people can switch on or switch off T.V. sets according to their convenience and requirement. Cable T.V. telecasts many programmes which are very useful for children and students. Many academic programmes are telecast on Cable T.V. and students according to their academic requirements, can derive maximum benefits from such programmes. Adults can switch off T.V. sets when some guest drops in. Watching T.V. is not more important than meeting a person or having a general talk or discussion with a guest. Children who are more curious to watch 'movies only for adults' can be dealt with strictly. It depends on the viewers how they make use of the programmes. Hence it is not the Cable T.V. which is to be blamed but the viewers who are not aware of their duties and responsibilities and continue to glue to their T.V. sets.

Everything in this universe has two sides—positive and negative. It is for us to avoid the negative and adopt the positive. Similarly, we can avoid watching such programmes on Cable T.V. which disturb our peace of mind or which corrupt ours or our children's minds.

Thus, we cannot blame Cable T.V. just for the sake of criticism. We can surely adopt, watch and assimilate what is good for us and avoid what is harmful for us.

Sir, I therefore strongly and emphatically declare that Cable T.V. is not a nuisance but a good source of information, entertainment and education.

❑ ❑ ❑

Pen is Mightier Than the Sword

A. Debator in Favour of the Motion

Mr Chairman, sir

There is no doubt that pen is all powerful. Whatever can be achieved by an educated person, cannot be achieved by a person who is strong in terms of physical strength but low in intellect. All persons who rose to the greatest heights of their lives were largely those people who were abundantly endowed with the power of pen. They were peaceful, calm and had the qualities of patience and perseverance.

A physically strong person who boasts of his body leads a wrong life and suffers in the end. Bodily strength is not very helpful in achieving something great in life. However, he, who is educated, well-read and intellectual, does not brag about his qualities, achieves great success in life. He remains happy and successful throughout his life.

Pen is certainly more powerful than sword. This world would soon come to an end if sword is made to supersede the pen. The mighty armies of the world can annihilate all humanity if the role of pen is neglected. Only educated citizens of all countries of the world prevent fights, quarrels, battles and wars. If sword is considered all powerful, there would be no peace in the world. Physical strength is nothing before the mental strength. An educated person possesses all the qualities of head and heart whereas an uneducated person, though physically strong, is always ready to pick up quarrels and show his body power. All good things on this earth are the gifts of pen. Sword can only shed blood. Pen can win the hearts of the people. Love begets love. Sword creates hatred and ill-will among the fellow beings. Nothing can be gained with the help of sword. One may be mistaken to think that sword is more powerful. It can kill and destroy. On the other hand, one may feel that pen is a useless thing but it has great power. It has the power to change the society without causing any violence and bloodshed. It can change the pattern of thinking of society, and the mindset of people. It can bring about a revolution without any uproar. History is replete with examples when pen caused revolution in society. For example, the French Revolution of 1789, which was caused by the power of pen, is largely attributed to great scholars of contemporary society.

However, if one thinks deeply, one may understand that what can be gained with the help of a pen, can never be gained by a sword.

Sir, I firmly believe that the pen is more powerful than the power of sword.

B. Debator Against the Motion

Mr Chairman, sir

My worthy friend who spoke before me was all praise for pen. He is of the opinion that pen is stronger than sword.

However, I strongly believe that it is the sword which is all powerful and which can win all battles. What a sword can do, pen cannot do. Had pen been mightier than sword, there would have been no need of armies. All the countries of the world try to have powerful army, airforce and naval powers. If educated persons only sit inside offices and discuss various issues and draw strategies, nothing can be achieved. It is the sword which wins battles and deters the enemy.

Since the dawn of history, all battles and wars in the world were fought with force. No pen played its role. We all have heard the saying 'if we want peace, we should always be prepared for war'. Those who are physically weak say that pen is stronger than sword. Countries who had weak armies were attacked by their enemy countries. As a result, the defeated countries tried to strengthen their armed forces and accumulated weapons of mass destruction. It is the sword which keeps the enemy at bay. Pen cannot help in this situation. It is only the army which helps. Pen is a weak weapon, rather it is no weapon at all. The fear of the sword is all powerful.

People who take the help of pen and try to create peaceful communities and societies are considered weak and always have the risk of being attacked and subdued by the stronger forces.

Whether it is a fight between two individuals, two groups or two countries, it is the sword that decides the fate of the party.

I fail to understand how a pen can win battles and how it can prevent wars. It is the sword which is the ultimate winner and hence the role of sword cannot be underestimated.

Sir, I therefore emphatically declare that pen is not mightier than sword but it is the sword which is the mightiest of all.

Death Penalty Should Be Abolished

A. Debator in Favour of the Motion

Mr Chairman, sir

I strongly favour the motion that death penalty should be abolished. Today, we live in a civilised society and therefore death penalty should be abolished completely.

In spite of the fact that death penalty is still in practice in many countries of the world, the rate of crime has not decreased. Even the hardened criminals cannot be reformed if death punishment is prevalent. Death punishment creates more hatred and a feeling of revenge.

Rather reformative and rehabilitative approach should be taken to bring about a change in the life of the criminals. They should be treated with love and compassion. If criminals are jailed for some time according to the gravity of their crimes it offers them an opportunity to repent for their misdeeds and try to reform themselves.

About two-thirds countries have already abolished capital punishment by law and twenty more have it on statute. These twenty countries have not used it at all for several years. Thus, death penalty does not exist in about 100 countries. India is one of the 80-odd countries which have retained it. Capital punishment provided in the Indian Penal Code has failed to check the increase in homicides over the years.

The American Bill of Rights in the Eighth Amendment did prohibit "Cruel and Unusual Punishment", and the Fifth Amendment forbade the government from taking any life without due process of law. The case abolishing the death penalty rests mainly on the traditional ground cited; namely, that it has not been decisively proved that such penalty deters crime. The same research points out that the impact is just marginal and for short periods only. It is also said that an overwhelming number of those executed as in the case of the U.S. come from the poorest sections of the society. Also, there is apprehension in some countries that death sentences are biased against certain racial minorities. One of the arguments that holds strong ground is that the prosecution and judges are not infallible and can and do mistakes. Here such a mistake can prove irrevocable.

The factor that gross injustice could be done to totally innocent persons or those guilty of offences that do not amount to a first-degree murder is itself sufficiently significant to abolish death sentence. The criminal justice system all over the world is overloaded. The poor and illiterate defendants generally do not have access to adequate legal assistance. Nor do they get the breaks which the rich get—like long years passing between the occurrence of crime and actual trial, surety for bail, and other aids to walk free. Numerous cases of custodial deaths have been coolly pushed under the carpet, or the perpetrators let off with what is described as a light slap on the wrist.

As the poor cannot afford huge sums for bails nor eminent lawyers, who can use every trick in the books to defend their clients, they are subjected to the full rigours of the law. Judges also often decide cases on a discriminatory or arbitrary basis without sufficient checks on their powers.

When a state convicts prisoners without affording them a fair trial, it denies them the right to seek legal redress for wrongful conviction. Irrevocable death sentence removes not only the victim's right to seek legal redress for wrongful conviction, but also the judicial system's capacity to correct its errors.

A fair trial must mean a trial where the defendant has full opportunities, taking the social and economic factors into consideration.

The "rarest of rare" death sentence and executions fall mostly on the poorest of the poor or those who have no access to good legal aid and who may necessarily not be deserving that which is meted out to them. And that is one very strong reason to abolish death penalty.

Sir, I, therefore, strongly declare that death penalty should be abolished.

B. Debator Against the Motion

Mr Chairman, sir

I have a difference of opinion with my friend who emphatically declared that death penalty should be abolished from all countries of this world. If death penalty is completely abolished, virtually a hell will be let loose on this earth.

The crime rate is sure to rise if capital punishment is abolished. People will have no fear of the law. Even now when death penalty still exists in most of the countires, many criminals commit heinous crimes in the hope that their lawyers will be able to let them off with a little punishment. If death penalty is abolished, nothing will be left to deter the criminals.

Most of the people with a criminal bent of mind commit

crimes and feel proud. Being ruffians and criminals give them a feeling of joy and superiority. The fear of death penalty is the greatest deterrent. When criminals come to know that some accused was hanged for a serious offence, they try to control their tempers and sometimes completely give up criminal life.

Reforms have failed to stop crimes. Soft and lenient punishments have encouraged criminals to commit more and more crimes. Hard-core criminals will not give up committing serious crimes unless very stringent punishments are given to them. All the methods of soft treatment to the criminals to abandon their life of crime all over the world, have failed to check the crime rate. It is the highest punishment—death penalty—that can bring down the crime rate to a greater extent.

British America reported an execution as early as in 1608 when in Virginia, an ex-Councillor was hanged for betrayal of the colony to Spain. In 1632, a woman was executed for the first time. Several other colonies including New York, New England, Pennsylvania had the death sentence in their statutes well before the First Congress met in 1790 to adopt the U.S. Constitution that provided for the death penalty for rape and first-degree murder.

In 1976 the U.S. Supreme Court in Gregy v/s Georgia case upheld a new capital punishment law that remedied the affirmities pointed out in the Furman case. The year also witnessed several other rulings of the court upholding that the death penalty was in order as long as it was not arbitrary and was imposed after observing the due process of law.

In sum, the U.S. Supreme Court sees no basic objection to death penalty and the same is the case in many other countries. The U.S. is often projected by retentionists as an example of a tough country that has demonstrated the effectiveness of the capital punishment in controlling violent crime.

The above cited examples confirm to the fact that capital punishment can be a great deterrent against the rising graph of crime particularly in India where despite sufficient legal provisions people do not hesitate to commit even henious crime. Somewhere in their mind they are sure that they would hire efficient lawyers who would definitely save them from punishment. Indeed, it is its effectiveness in crime control that has led to continue it in a developed country like America. Hence it should never be abolished in India.

Sir, I therefore strongly feel that death sentence should not be abolished.

❑ ❑ ❑

Child Labour is the Biggest Problem of the World

A. Debator in Favour of the Motion

Mr Chairman, sir

There is no doubt that child labour is one of the biggest socio-economic problems of the world. Child labour is mainly the upshot of poverty, unemployment and illiteracy. In fact, it is the perpetrator of these maladies. Unless the child labour is eradicated, the world's progress in the present millennium is bound to be poor. Every year we celebrate Human Rights Day and talk big about human rights of every individual. Big announcements are made to check the violation of human rights. On this occasion, discussions, seminars are held and pledges taken to eradicate the menace of child labour. But for the children of the world who languish in slavery in dimly lit, cramped spaces in factories, houses, toiling 16 hours a day, getting little pay and more abuse—life continues as usual. Slavery was one of the first human rights issue to arouse widespread concern at international levels. Although our civilisation has entered 21st century, child labour continues as the worst form of slavery in society.

According to the latest census reports, of the 200 million Indian children in the age of 5-14, about 11.3 million are labourers. However, non-official sources embarrassingly reveal that there are, in fact, over 60 million child labourers in India working in various industries such as carpet, bangle, matches, fireworks, brassware, pottery and brick kiln units and as domestic helps. The carpet industry has 300,000 children working for it.

The irony is that these children who sell their labour to an employer in lieu of the wages have no identity as workers. They have to just obey their master and remain at their mercy. There are no minimum wages or fixed working hours for them. Vulnerable to physical and mental exploitation, the children are abused, beaten, sexually exploited and more often than not such abuses go unnoticed. This is really a blot on the modern civil society.

The complex issue of child labour is a developmental issue. It cannot be eliminated by focussing on the determinant like education or enforcement of child labour laws unless the needs of the poor are fulfilled. It greatly hamper the development of India as a nation. Children grow up illiterate for they have been working when they have to be in school. It forms a vicious cycle of poverty and the need for child labour is reborn generation after generation.

Despite the umpteen laws safeguarding the rights of the child, and the UN Declaration of Human Rights, and Convention on the Rights of the Child, aimed at ensuring healthy growth and holistic development of children, the problem of child labour has risen to menacing proportions. The main hurdle in the abolition of child labour lies in the enforcement of the law apart from the laws themselves which are full of loopholes and are anomalous. Moreover, the Government of India must ensure that the needs of the poor are fulfilled before attacking the problem of child labour. If the poverty is addressed, the need for child labour will automatically decline.

Sir, I therefore fully support the motion that child labour is the biggest problem of the world.

B. Debator Against the Motion

Mr Chairman, sir

My worthy friend who spoke before me emphatically declared that child labour is the biggest problem of the world.

However, I am of the view that there are many more serious and glaring problems in the world than child labour. Poverty, unemployment, overpopulation and pollution are more serious problems in the world.

Child labour is not at all the menacing problem. It is, in fact, a source of income for the poor families. Poor parents who have many children, cannot feed them, clothe them and educate them properly. They have to get their children employed in factories, shops, homes or somewhere else so as to earn money for the family. Child labour, which we call a problem is, indeed, a source of support to his family. Children get employment and are thus able to earn some money to feed their poor parents and siblings. If there is no child labour, poor families would starve.

Certainly, children essentially work to maintain the economic level of the households, either in the form of work of wages, or help in household enterprises. In all the activities, the basic objective is to provide the family financial support. A child labour's income is important to the livelihood of a poor family. Since there are no social welfare systems in India as those in the West and no easy access to credit facility to the poor families, child labour is a great source of support to these families.

All laws and regulations framed by the governments of various countries have completely failed to check child labour. Undoubtedly, child labour is an unavoidable necessity. One can imagine the conditions of the poor families if children are not given employment. Child labour is the only solution to keep their world running.

The rich parents who can afford to educate their children have no necessity to get their children employed. The employment of children is not a compulsion for the rich parents. However, it is the necessity of the poor parents who have no source of livelihood. If they do not get their children employed, they would certainly starve and die.

Poverty, unemployment and overpopulation are the biggest problems in the world. If population is controlled, the problem of child labour will automatically get solved. If there are small families and less children, parents can feed them, clothe them and educate them properly. Child labour is, in fact, the offshoot of overpopulation. Similarly, if overpopulation is controlled, the problem of unemployment will get automatically solved.

Sir, I therefore strongly oppose the motion that child labour is the biggest problem of the world.

❑ ❑ ❑

Money is All Powerful

A. Debator in Favour of the Motion

Chairman, sir

I fully support the motion that money is all powerful. Money makes the mare go. Nothing can be done without money. Money can buy us all the necessities as well as luxuries of life. No one can survive on this earth without money. If a person does not have money, he cannot feed himself nor can he feed his family. Had money not been that important, no one would care to earn or have money.

All human beings are busy earning money. Some are employed either in public or private sector and some are busy earning money in their own business houses. The desire to earn and have money keeps everyone busy. If there is no requirement for money, life would become dull. It would lose all charms of life. The need for earning money is felt by one and all and this need only keeps all persons busy.

The more money a person has the better would be his standard of living. Without having adequate money one cannot buy the bare minimum necessities of daily requirement. Money is needed for food, clothes, house, education, marriage and for everything. If a person has more than enough money, he can lead a better and prosperous life.

Poor people are not able to make even their both ends meet what to talk of living in luxurious or prosperous life-style. Money keeps all the worries and cares away.

People who have sufficient money need not bother about their food, house, clothes and better education to their children or spending money on the marriages of their children. People having no money or not enough money are always surrounded by worries and anxieties about educating their children and finding the right matches for their sons or daughters. In fact, nothing stirs without money.

In India and in developing countries as well lots of people die for want of proper medical care. Though there are latest technologies to cure deadly diseases, unfortunately, a great number of people do not have accessibility to these facilities. They do not have money to afford the expenses of the treatment. At the same time malnutrition is also a big health related issue. This is the result of the insufficient intake of balanced nutritious diets. About one-fourth of the total population of India live below poverty line. they find it difficult to make their both ends meet, what to talk about nutritious diet.

Sir, I, therefore, strongly support the motion that money is all powerful.

B. Debator Against the Motion

Chairman, sir

My worthy friend who spoke before me strongly declared that money is all powerful.

I, however, strongly oppose the motion that money is all powerful. Only the Almighty is all powerful. He can turn kings into paupers and paupers into king overnight. Money never remains with one person. It keeps on changing hands. Very rich persons become very poor and very poor persons become rich.

If one nurses the opinion that it is the money which is all powerful one is greatly mistaken. If our deeds are righteous, money will automatically come. But if one has love only for money and what money can buy, one is sure to suffer. Money is just needed to satisfy our bare minimum needs. It cannot buy all pleasures of life.

Money is not God. If one is God-fearing, religious-minded and does not resort to ignoble means to earn money, money will stay with him. However, money earned through ignoble means will surely slip from the hands of the earners very soon. If one is devoted to God and does righteous deeds, he need not worry about money. It will surely be with him to meet his daily needs. Money cannot provide health. People who accumulate a lot of money, become haughty and arrogant. They suffer from many physical and mental maladies. They cannot enjoy good food because their physicians advise them not to eat this or that due to some health-related problems.

In fact, money is the root cause of many troubles. Most of the problems existing on this earth are attributed to the greed for money. No one can eat money. It is a useless things for animals. They need grass, flesh or their natural food. How can money be all powerful? Money makes friends enemies and creates friction and ill-will among close relations.

If a poor person gets a lot of money and becomes rich, he is deprived of the qualities of compassion, sympathy and fellow-feelings and starts hating the poor people, forgetting that he was also poor once. Money never solves the problems, rather it adds to the problems.

The greed for having more and more money is responsible for all the maladies afflicting the world. People desire to accumulate more and more money thereby have become selfish, self-centred and cheat. They have forgotten about all the good human values which are more important than money. They can go to any extent to earn more and more money. A few years ago, values were more dear to people than money and they possessed all the qualities of head and heart.

Unfortunately, today all values have been thrown to winds and the greed for money has become the sole target of life and is responsible for many of our social problems.

Sir, I, therefore strongly oppose the motion that money is all powerful.

❑ ❑ ❑

NOTES

NOTES